PERFECT WAVE

PERFECT WAVE

REFLECTING GOD BY PROTECTING THE EARTH

COY LINDSEY

{UNDERCURRENT SERIES}

Barefoot Ministries®
Kansas City, Missouri

Copyright 2008 by Barefoot Ministries®

ISBN 978-0-8341-5026-3

Printed in the United States of America

Editor: Mike Wonch
Assistant Editor: Catherine M. Shaffer
Cover Design: Lindsey Rohner
Interior Design: Sharon Page

All Scripture quotations are from the *Holy Bible, New American Standard Bible*® (NASB®). Copyright
© 1960, 1962, 1963, 1968, 1971, 1972, 1973,1975, 1977, 1995 by The Lockman Foundation.
Used by permission. (www.Lockman.org)

Library of Congress Control Number: 2008929042

10 9 8 7 6 5 4 3 2 1

ACKNOWLEDGMENTS

For Brooklyn and Kirra, who've taught me to love in ways I would have never imagined possible.

CONTENTS

INTRODUCTION
HOLY SURF

Less than 72 hours after our college graduation, Brooklyn (my wife) and I packed all of our belongings, including our new puppy named Chip, into a moving truck and drove toward a final destination of Orlando, Florida. The first 22 years of my life were spent enduring the freezing winters of southeast Ohio. Sunny Florida was our new home, and gone were the days of playing in the snow. Long, thick socks and heavy snow boots were soon replaced by flip-flops (the cheaper the better). In a few short months, my entire wardrobe changed. So did the majority of activities in my life.

Surfing! All it took was one trip to the beach with some friends and a surfboard, and I was hooked. My new favorite thing to do was to surf, even though the first day I couldn't even stay on the board lying down. I loved the feeling of lying on a fiberglass board pushing across the smooth, glass-like water. I may not have stood to my feet the first day, week, or even month that I started surfing, but I couldn't get enough of the sport. It wasn't long before I bought my first board. It was seven feet and eight inches of fun, custom shaped by a friend I met in seminary.

Everywhere I go to visit friends or family outside the state of Florida, I hear the same question: Are you a surfer? Maybe it's the combination of the way I dress and the fact that I live in Florida, but people normally jump to the conclusion that I must surf. It's a tricky question to answer, because I'm not totally sure what qualifies one to be worthy of the title "surfer." If it is the ability to ramp ten feet above a wave or drop in on a wave that towers 30 feet above my head, then no, I'm not a surfer (neither is most of the world). If a surfer is anyone who loves to spend time in the ocean riding a manufactured board on three to four foot waves, however, then count me in; I'm a surfer.

If you read this book with the hope that you'll learn all the tricks to riding the tube at Pipeline or catching air and turning a 360, you'll be greatly disappointed. I'm not that person. I'm not a competitive surfer, and you'll never find my name on the "world's top 40 surfers" list. I do love the sport, though, and it has given me many hours of frustration, fun, and freedom.

Moving to Florida brought together two worlds that by most people's standard should never be joined: surfing and Christianity. Less than 30 years ago, surfing had a bad reputation. You could say it still does, but it used to be much worse. During the 1950s, '60s and '70s, surfers were associated with teenage boys who rebelled against society's rules. Surfers were stereotyped as lazy, substance-abusing, girl-chasing losers who contributed little to the well-being of the world. In other words, surfers weren't considered good people. Like you would expect, because some Christians don't want their children to hang around bad people, the world of surfing and the world of Christianity didn't mix. They were considered to be polar opposites.

Though the two worlds of surfing and Christianity seemed to be moving in opposite directions 30 years ago, they began moving toward each other and eventually collided at the intersection of my life. Surfing met God and God met surfing, and they've shared some great conversations. God used surfing and seminary to teach me something that was missing from my understanding of a holy life.

Through my experiences with surfing, God helped me realize that caring for creation is part of what it means to be a Christian. It is a way to reflect the perfect image of God, to be the person God wants me to be. It's not optional or a special concern of some, it's something that all Christians are called to do. God is calling us to take care of the created world as a way to reflect God's image. Living a holy life includes doing everything that we can to look after the wellbeing of God's creation, earth.

I know I've used the word "holy" a couple times and maybe it's seems somewhat confusing, but actually it's really simple. The word "holy" means "set apart" or "made separate" by God to accomplish God's special purpose for your life. For those who accept Christ, God has designed an entirely different way of living than the rest of the world. God changes the way you see things which changes the way you do things, and so you end up living a life that is "set apart" or different from those who have yet to accept Christ. One thing that God wants to change about the way we see things and act is how we treat our planet. Holiness includes the actions we take to care for God's good creation.

Okay, at this point, you might be thinking I'm crazy. There's a good possibility that you might think I'm saying the same thing that a host of celebrities or politicians have said. It's all over the place; everybody's talking about going green. I'm not saying you need to go green or protect the environment because it's the cool thing to do or because science says the world will end soon if we don't. I'm not trying to convince you of an argument just so you'll be on my side of the debate. No, I'm only telling you what God has taught me about living a life that is pleasing to Him. God wants us to care for creation, and in doing so, we start to look more like the person God desires us to be, which is a reflection of His image.

I never anticipated the impact moving to Florida and learning to surf would have on my own spiritual life. It's not that I abused the environment or despised people who talked about protecting the earth; it was a topic that I just didn't think was important to my relationship with God. I'd never heard a pastor preach on the importance of caring for creation, and most of the people I knew labeled any person who talked about the environment a "tree hugger." Surfing brought me literally face to face with creation, and God took it as an opportunity to open my eyes to another way that I'm called to live a holy life.

That's what you'll find in this book. You'll read the thoughts of an average surfer who encountered God in a new way and learned that being a Christian involves caring for the earth. Just like reading the Bible, worshipping God at church, praying for God's will and loving my neighbor are all important, taking care of God's good earth is a part of our spiritual growth process. I hope you join me in the journey to discover what it means to live a holy life as I explain using my experiences with surfing.

SECTION ONE
SEARCH FOR PERFECTION

The ultimate goal of every surfer is to find and surf the perfect wave. Deep in the heart of every person who's ever surfed is an insatiable desire to discover perfection and ride down the face of it. Like little children at Christmas who have visions of sugarplums dancing in their heads, a surfer anxiously awaits the day when the ocean will swell up into a flawless form of beauty and power. It's a craving that drives all of us to do crazy things, and some of us have the scars and credit card bills to prove it.

It all begins the first time you catch a wave. I can still remember the first time I caught a wave (I mean really stood up and rode the line). There's a difference between standing up on a surfboard the size of a mini-boat and riding it straight into shore and using a shorter board and riding it down the beach. You've probably seen people catch a wave that looked like white water rapids was chasing them straight to the beach, that's not what I'm talking about. When someone truly stands up and rides the line, it looks like the person is barely one second ahead of the wave crashing on their head as it chases the surfer either up or down the beach. That's what I remember the first time I was able to ride parallel to the beach rather perpendicular with it.

The day it happened, I was surfing with Brandon. I was watching Brandon catch waves right and left all day while I worked as I hard as I could to ride one or two waves an hour straight into the beach. The beach where we were surfing was a spot for beginners and mediocre surfers. In other words, it was perfect for me. Other than Brandon and a few other people, all the other surfers were struggling just like me, but then the breakthrough occurred. Finally, my timing was right and my muscles made the right movement. As I stood up and looked forward, I realized that for the first time, I was riding parallel to the beach rather than straight at it. As I looked back, I realized the wave was chasing me, hoping to swallow me up like the big fish that swallowed Jonah. I screamed at Brandon, "Did you see me? Did you see me catch that wave and ride it down the line?" It was at that moment in time that the hunger pangs for a *perfect wave* first became real to me.

I think I mentioned earlier that a desire to find and surf the perfect wave causes some of us to do crazy things. Well, I'm guilty. You may remember the hurricanes that devastated Florida in the late summer or early fall of 2004. If not, let me recap: Four powerful hurricanes slammed into the coast of Florida in less than two months, and two of them decided to take almost the same path. Growing up in Ohio didn't equip me with proper survival skills. I'd never even heard of hurricane shutters until all of my neighbors started screwing them into the outside of their houses to protect the windows. Everyone was fleeing our town and most of the state, so we did the best we knew how and drove to shelter on the west coast of Florida. It wasn't the best choice, because the hurricane still succeeded in maintaining enough strength to eliminate electrical power where we were staying all the way across the state.

It was like a dream driving through our hometown the day after the hurricane had passed. Trees were down, debris was everywhere, all power was lost, and the majority of the people still hadn't come home. It was a ghost town, but with palm trees instead of tumbleweeds. Within minutes, the initial shock was over, and I was already thinking about surfing again. Florida doesn't get the biggest and best waves compared to California or Hawaii, which means most of the time we rely on storms to produce waves. It didn't take long for the light bulb to come on in my head. What could be more powerful and capable of creating a big wave than a hurricane?

I called Brandon immediately and told him my idea, and before I knew it, we loaded our boards and headed for the beach. Up to this point, I had only seen hurricane damage about ten miles inland, which was a nightmare to see. When we made it beachside and drove down A1A, I came face to face with the true devastation caused by swirling winds in excess of 100 mph. I will never forget the image of the Baptist church we always drove by on the way to the beach. The steeple had completely broken off the top of the building and stabbed a hole in the center of the sanctuary roof. Everything looked so different; it almost felt like we were in a foreign place.

The destruction didn't stop us, because we only had one thing in mind: taking advantage of hurricane-powered surf. The safest place to park my car was at a local surf shop across the street from the beach. Within seconds, we had our boards in hand and were weaving our way in and out of power lines as we headed for the beach. Every step was a gamble as broken glass and debris littered the street, not to mention electrical lines. Still, we focused on our purpose of finding the big waves.

All of this may sound insane, but I still haven't told you the crazy part yet. We carefully carried our boards through the nearly-collapsed mangrove tunnel that took us to the beach, and as we crested the walkway, we caught our first look. The best way I know how to describe what we saw is a washing machine. Imagine the movement and flow of the water in a washing machine, and now imagine the ocean waters doing the same thing. The waves were big, they were messy, they were powerful, and they were breaking everywhere and in every direction as far as we could see. There wasn't a surfer in sight, but we didn't get that far to go home dry, so we secured our leashes around our ankles and started paddling out.

Luckily, the conditions were so bad that I couldn't paddle out far enough to catch a big wave. As soon as I'd gain a little distance, a wave would crash right in front of me and drag me back to where I started. Even still, I was determined to get out there and find the perfect wave. An hour went by, and I was still getting pounded by wave after wave. We decided to give up. While I was pouring my heart and soul out to make it past the inside break, I didn't realized that I had drifted about a mile up the beach. Brandon and I got out of the water and didn't even know where we were, and the only choice was to start walking. It was a long, sad walk back to the car. Looking back, I realize my desire to ride the perfect wave had caused me to do something so crazy it could have easily taken my life. I was driven to perfection.

What I'm about to say may sound strange or even crazy, especially considering the story I just told you, but stay with me. Like surfing, the ultimate goal of the Christian life is perfection. Every person who has accepted Christ begins searching for the same thing, a God-given perfection. Deep in the heart of every person who's called Jesus "Savior" is a desire to be like Christ. Every moment of every day, all one can think about is the day when God's love completely fills one's heart and expels all imperfections.

Perfection is a heavy word. It seems impossible that any person could be totally perfect, at least as we understand the word. Christian perfection is a hard concept to grasp, but imagine if people never changed after they became Christians. Imagine if people asked for forgiveness, but continued living the same life they'd always lived. It wouldn't make sense; Christians wouldn't be different from anyone else. Accepting Christ would simply be an easy ticket to heaven, and what we did on earth wouldn't matter.

God sent Jesus not only so we would be forgiven of our sins, but also so the power of sin in our lives could be overcome. The moment you first believe in God is the same moment that God starts working in your life to help you overcome sin. When you ask God to enter your heart, God comes in and starts changing you into a new person who is no longer under the dominance of sin. As long as you allow Him room, God continues to kick out all of the ugliness of sin and replaces it with the beauty of love. As sin in your life is replaced with love, the way you live your life begins to look more like the way Jesus lived His life. If you let Him, God will continue to exchange the sin in your heart with love until one day all that remains is love. This is perfection, the goal of Christianity, that some day God would fill every corner of our hearts with love. To be made perfect is to have a heart that is pure love and, in everything, to reflect that love.

Don't be fooled or misled, perfection isn't about following a long list of rules. I admit, I used to think that being perfect meant being able to check off all the boxes next to all the rules. It didn't take long for me to realize that you don't need love to follow a rule, because I knew a lot of people who followed a lot of the rules but didn't have love. Following the rules isn't the goal of perfection; love is. You don't follow rules to achieve perfection. Instead, you live a certain way because you're being made perfect. Perfection is love motivating you to do what is right.

I wish I could tell you that the insatiable desire to be made perfect doesn't cause Christians to do crazy things, but I wouldn't be telling you the truth. For people who don't have a relationship with God, what Christians do who are being made perfect does seem crazy. It seems crazy to others that people would love others more than themselves, care for the sick, help the poor, praise God with loud music or quiet prayers, follow the words of an ancient book (the Bible), love their enemy, and yes, even care for this earth. In the quest for perfection, love requires us to do many crazy things.

One crazy thing that love requires, which you'll find on the front and back of all the pages in this book, is caring for God's creation. If you've accepted Christ and a desire to be filled with love is burning deep inside you, then a part of that decision is recognizing the call God places on us to take care of His created world. To do otherwise is to deny God's purpose for your life, which is to make you perfect. Denying God's purpose is an easy way to stunt your growth toward perfection, which means love isn't able to fill up your heart the way it should. Part of the path toward perfection is understanding your relationship with God's creation.

I don't know if this is a new thought for you, but it definitely was something new for me to consider. Growing up in church, I thought I'd learned everything I needed to know about being a Christian. I was taught to read my Bible, go to church, say my prayers, and love my neighbor. It wasn't until surfing brought me into personal contact with the beauty and wonder of the earth's ocean, however, that I realized my responsibility to care for creation. In the same way God expects me to do the other things I learned growing up in church, God also desires that I treat the earth with care.

Some people, including Christians, laugh at the idea that it matters to God how we treat the earth. They think we're going crazy and start calling us names like "hippie" or "tree-hugger." They might accuse us of supporting a certain political view, or they might blow us off as a radical thinker who will someday grow up and forget petty issues such as caring for the earth. They can be as loud as they want with their opinions, but the truth will never change; it matters to God how we treat creation.

The ultimate goal of every true believer in Jesus Christ is—or at least should be—perfection, which is a heart filled only with love. God begins filling our hearts with love the moment we say yes to God's will for our lives. God shapes and molds us into a new creation until all sin is removed and all that remains is love. As our hearts begin to fill up with love, we start to think and act differently. One area in which love influences us to live differently is our relationship with God's creation, earth.

CHAPTER 1
WHAT IS ENVIRONMENTAL HOLINESS?

The brief, yet complicated, way to summarize the main idea of this book in two words is Environmental Holiness. It's complicated because it combines two words that seemingly have no connection, and one of the words is hardly a part of our everyday language. At least I don't know many young people who go on and on about the subject of "holiness." To be fair, I don't have many friends past the student age who use or understand the word holiness. If you don't have a clue what "Environmental Holiness" means, no problem; you'll find out in the next few pages.

We learned earlier that the ultimate goal of every Christian, like every surfer, is perfection. Perfection is what God does in us to remove sin from our lives and fill our hearts with love, so that everything we do is motivated by love. Well, holiness is the process of God making us perfect.

I also mentioned that when God begins to replace the sin in our lives with love, we start to think and act differently. Our actions change to reflect the change in our hearts. One area in our hearts and lives which God begins to change is how we care for creation.

When I say "Environmental Holiness," it's a simple statement that God calls every Christian to care for creation as a part of the process of being made perfect. If we are searching for perfection, then we must be willing to let God change our thoughts and actions toward the environment. In the process of being made perfect, we start to reflect the perfect image of God.

CHAPTER 2
LOOK-A-LIKE
REFLECTING GOD'S IMAGE

Since Brooklyn graduated from college, she has been a full-time youth pastor. I don't know if it was by choice or default, but I have spent many hours with middle school and high school students. Spending so much time with students had its benefits. One of the benefits was borrowing their stuff, and believe me, I was a poor seminary student, so I definitely took advantage of it.

I never really asked to borrow the students' possessions, at least not until they offered. It didn't take long before one of Brooklyn's students, John, invited me to go surfing. "Yes" slipped out of my mouth before I even had a chance to think it, and we scheduled a day to make the hour drive over to Cocoa Beach. It was my very first surf adventure, and there's no doubt it turned out to be an adventure.

I hadn't lived in Orlando very long, which means I hadn't taken many trips to the beach. For the first 22 years of my life, the only experience I had with water sports was jumping off the diving board at our local swimming pool. I didn't grow up a surfer with a closet full of surfer clothing. I had one pair of swimming trunks, at least that's what I called them, and that was it. They were the type of swimwear that had the mesh material, like underwear made of fishnet, sewn to the inside of the shorts. Swim trunks were the cool thing in Ohio, but apparently not in Florida.

I showed up at John's house wearing my red and black swimming trunks with a tropical flower design all ready to go. John didn't warn me that he'd be wearing an in-style pair of long, baggy boardshorts made specifically for surfing. Nobody let me in on the secret that the surf world had come up with their own design and technology for shorts, which was the only cool way to go to the beach. Standing next to John, my swim trunks looked like a piece of clothing that belonged in a museum.

John in his stylish boardshorts and I in my grandpa-like swim trunks finally made it to the beach in about an hour. I didn't know anything about the Cocoa Beach Pier, but that's where we decided to park the car and unload the boards. It definitely was not the ideal place to show up pretending to be a surfer, especially considering my shorts gave me away. There were hundreds of people scattered everywhere: lying on the beach, fishing off the pier, playing beach volleyball, buying yummy food, and surfing. All of them seemed to fit the scene, and then there was me.

The excitement about the fact that I was about to attempt surfing for the first time overshadowed the embarrassment that I looked like I belonged on a cruise ship playing shuffleboard. It didn't matter to me what I looked like, I was focused on getting in the water. I slapped the sunscreen on the best I could and headed for the waves.

Did I forget to mention that John only had one surfboard? If you were wondering, no, two people cannot ride one surfboard at the same time. We had to take turns riding John's only board. To make matters worse, John's board was a short board. Short boards, which usually are not much bigger than six feet, are designed for experienced surfers who are looking for more speed and the ability to make quick turns and perform crazy tricks. Long boards, on the other hand, are normally around ten feet long and are designed for any level surfer who is looking for a slower, smoother ride down the face of a wave. Basically, John's board was one of the most difficult boards to ride.

I spent most of the day learning how to stay on the board and actually move somewhere instead of looking like a dead fish floating in the water. Needless to say, it was a long, unsuccessful day; I didn't stand up one time. I'm sure it was obvious to everyone else on the beach and in the water that day that I wasn't a surfer—I didn't look or act like a surfer. I did not reflect the image of a surfer.

Like the first day I went surfing with John, most of us start the Christian life unaware of what it means to think, look, or act like the people God is calling us to be. It's okay, though, because in the same moment that God forgives us of our sins, He starts working in our lives to fill our hearts with love and remove all imperfections. In the process of being made perfect, we begin to reflect the image of God, and what is more perfect than the image of God?

When I say the image of God, I'm not saying that you need to have shoulder length hair, grow some sort of beard, wear a white robe with a purple sash and replace all your shoes with authentic, hand-crafted leather sandals. That's not what it means to reflect the image of God.

I don't know if you've heard, but God created humans in His image. I'm not lying; it says so in Genesis 1:26-27:

> "Then God said, 'Let us make man in Our image, according to Our likeness; and let them rule over the fish of the sea and over the birds of the sky and over the cattle and over all the earth, and over every creeping thing that creeps on the earth.' God created man in His own image, in the image of God He created him; male and female He created them."

Isn't it crazy to think that in the beginning God created us in such a way that we reflected His own image and were made perfectly? From the moment Adam and Eve first took a breath, they were exactly the way God intended us to be. Before they even started living, they had already arrived; they had the capacity to think and act like God would think and act. They didn't need to grow and mature into the people God was calling them to be, because that's who they already were. God's original design for humanity was a creation made in His image.

In Genesis 1:26-28, we learn that to be made in the image of God means that we are like God in our abilities and responsibilities, especially concerning our relationship with the earth. Adam and Eve were to care for or "rule over the fish of the sea and over the birds of the sky and over the cattle and over *all the earth*" (emphasis added). God's original plan was for humanity to partner with Him by giving us the opportunity to rule over the earth. However, with the ability to rule came a responsibility. Because it was a partnership with God, the responsibility was to rule over the earth in the same way that God would rule the earth.

Though it's true that God created humanity in His image, it's also true that the image in us has been distorted by sin. Adam and Eve were perfect until they listened to the serpent and disobeyed God's command. When they ate from the forbidden tree, an act against the will of God, sin entered their hearts and messed up who they were created to be. Now, the abilities and responsibilities of the image of God are easily confused with the lures of sin. Because of Adam and Eve's sin, the image of God in every human being is in need of restoration.

God originally created humans in His image. The image is still there, but sin warps the way we think, act, and live. We need God to transform us into people who reflect the image of perfection as we once did. Holiness is what happens when God enters our lives and begins repairing the damage; it is the process of being made perfect.

Environmental Holiness is God restoring the part of the image that gives us the ability and responsibility to care for creation, the earth. It is opening our eyes to the partnership God made with humanity in the beginning, that we would "rule over the earth" in God's stead. When we allow God to move in our lives, our view of creation begins to change from a perspective that sees the earth as something to be consumed for our own pleasure, to a perspective that sees creation as something in need of our help to ensure its protection and well-being. Environmental Holiness is God making us perfect in our relationship with earth.

The first day I went surfing, I didn't look like a surfer. I didn't even know what it meant to dress like a surfer, and I definitely had no chance of fooling anyone with my skills, or lack thereof, in the water. Early in our relationship with God, many of us face the same plight; we don't look like the image of God, and for the most part, we don't know what it means to reflect it—especially concerning our treatment of the earth. Thankfully, with both surfing and the reflecting the image of God, there's plenty of opportunity for growth. The difference is, the success of our surfing lies with what we can do as individuals, and restoring us to perfection lies in the hands of a loving and never-failing God.

CHAPTER 3
RASH GUARD
CARING FOR GOD'S EARTH

Surfing is different than any other sport I've experienced for one reason: surfers don't want anyone else to learn to surf. It sounds funny considering how many thousands of miles of beach exist, but it's all about crowd control. Local surfers don't like to share their waves. New surfers equal more crowds, which is a surfer's nightmare. (A surfers' dream would be to have the ocean all to one's self and two or three close friends on a day when the waves were perfect.) Because locals don't want new surfers to create more crowds, it's an unspoken agreement that surfers don't teach anyone else to surf. It's every man or woman for himself or herself. Even with the simplest things, it's up to you to learn through trial and error.

One of the first things I learned as a surfer was the purpose of wax. It's literally a small stick or bar of wax. It seems small and insignificant, but wax is probably the most important component to successful surfing, other than the shape of the board. It's with you wherever you go in the water—tucked away in a nifty little pocket inside your boardshorts. To be without wax would be like an ice skater whose skates were without blades; there's not much of a chance you'll stand on your feet very long.

The purpose of wax is to create traction for your body so you don't slip off the board. Before a surf session, every surfer applies a sensible amount of wax to their board. The amount of wax you apply depends on the size of the board and whether or not the board has traction pads. Needless to say, wax keeps you from slipping all over the board.

I learned how to apply wax in no time. However, it took me longer to learn the power of wax. I'd seen pictures of professional surfers wearing shirts in the water and honestly thought it was a preference of style for some, and protection for their skin from the sun's rays. It's not that I was way off base with those assumptions, but there was another reason for wearing a shirt. The hint should have been in the name of these shirts; they're called "rashguards."

Some things you just can't learn without experience, which is the way I learned how they got the name rashguards. I did an amazing job putting wax on my board. I could paddle hard, sit up straight while waiting on the next set (it's not easy to sit still without tipping over), and gain proper footing when attempting to stand up without the worry of slipping. It was beautiful weather, and the waves were in excellent form for learning, so I spent about four to five hours on my board.

I definitely learned the power of wax. Unfortunately, I didn't realize the wax would be subtly rubbing off the top layer of my skin all day long. When applied to the board, the wax sticks to the board in hundreds of tiny, jagged mounds, and to make matters worse, sand likes to work its way into the wax creating a sandpaper effect. I didn't notice this with my eyes. Besides, the determination to stand up at least once sort of numbed my body to any pain. My chest, stomach, arms, and legs took a beating for five hours. When I finally got out of the water, I looked like I had a bad sunburn from my chest to my stomach—everywhere else looked normal. It was like somebody dragged me on the carpet for hours, and I had the rug-burn—or wax-burn—to prove it. The next day, I woke up with scabs formed in the areas where the wax had rubbed me raw, and my skin was sensitive to the touch. It was then that I realized why they call it a rashguard: it guards your skin from the abuse of wax.

Up to this point, I've spoken of the side of Environmental Holiness that has to do with your own personal spiritual growth and well-being. I've connected caring for creation with the ability and responsibility that comes along with reflecting the image of God, which is what God does in us to make us perfect. There's another side to Environmental Holiness that also needs to be mentioned; it has to do with the growth and well-being of the earth. It's a different side because the focus is on creation and not on our own selves. Even before humanity's relationship with creation, God made earth and it was good. It has value because God made it that way, so this different side of Environmental Holiness calls us to care for and protect creation not only so we can be made perfect and good, but to restore the good to earth. Listen to God's opinion of earth:

"Then God said, 'Let the waters below the heavens be gathered into one place, and let the dry land appear;' and it was so. God called the dry land earth, and the gathering of the waters He called seas; and *God saw that it was good"* (Genesis 1:9-10, emphasis added).

"Then God said, 'Let the earth sprout vegetation, plants yielding seed, and fruit trees on the earth bearing fruit after their kind with seed in them'; and it was so. The earth brought forth vegetation, plants yielding seed after their kind, and trees bearing fruit with seed in them, after their kind; and *God saw that it was good"* (Genesis 1:11-12, emphasis added).

"Then God said, 'Let the waters teem with swarms of living creatures, and let birds fly above the earth in the open expanse of the heavens.' And God created the great sea monsters, and every living creature that moves, with which the waters swarmed after their kind, and every winged bird after its kind; and *God saw that it was good"* (Genesis 1:20-21, emphasis added)

God completed the earth in less than seven days, and at the end of each creation, God recognized it as good. God had no regrets, the earth and its environment was all good. Much like Adam and Eve were created in the image of God, the earth was created to be perfect. Also like Adam and Eve and the rest of humanity, the earth wasn't able to escape the damaging effects of sin.

Sin entered the world and started stealing away the goodness that once belonged to the created world. Sin disrupted the beauty and worth of creation and turned what was once good into something that is now struggling to survive. God's perfect creation is left vulnerable to the vandals of this world who deface the works of God's hand.

As people being recreated in the image of God, Christians have an opportunity to restore goodness to the earth. We are given a chance to protect and repair what God created to be perfect and good. In the same way that God is recreating us, we can take part in re-creating the earth. The earth is crying out for relief, and we can be part of the remedy.

My skin was not meant to endure hours of friction against a jagged, sticky surface. The end result was pain and damage, not to mention the embarrassment of walking up the beach looking like someone dragged me across the sand for a few miles. Similarly, the earth is not meant to endure the abuses and misuses inflicted on it by humanity. The result is wiping away the good God created, and if it's not stopped, the earth will be destroyed. My chest has a solution—a rashguard. The earth has a solution—you and me. Environmental Holiness isn't just about God perfecting us, it's also about us perfecting creation.

CHAPTER 4
MOVE TO THE EAST COAST
TAKING ACTION IS A MUST

For the first two years, our Florida address was Orlando. I loved where we lived and had no plans to move anywhere else, especially to a smaller town. Orlando offers the best of both worlds. It's less than an hour from Disney World and the beach. If I wanted to, I could go surf in the morning and hang out with Mickey and Minnie in the evening. What more could I ask for?

Well, life wasn't cooperating with my plans, and before I knew it, we were moving to the east coast. I couldn't get excited about the move, especially considering I still had a year left in seminary, which was about an hour drive one-way. In Orlando, we lived right next door to a brand new mall, movie theater, and state of the art fitness gym. I could walk over to buy a book, eat, catch a matinee movie, work out at the gym, and still have time to go home and swim. Life was good where I was, but the move was inevitable.

The only thing that caused any sense of joy when thinking of the move was the fact that we would live less than seven miles from the beach. Seven miles may seem far to you, but it wasn't to me considering it used to be a fifty-mile drive. Now, instead of planning an all-day weekend event at the beach three weeks ahead of time, I could be at the beach in less than ten minutes any day I wanted.

As you might imagine, my attitude about living on the east coast quickly began to change. I couldn't be upset about a morning surf session before church followed by a session after church, which was impossible in Orlando. I went from surfing once a month, or every other month, to surfing once or twice a week. Compared to a truly dedicated surfer, two days a week isn't much, but it was a huge increase in wave count for me. The more I surfed, the better I became.

My mind was made up, if I was going to live on the east coast of Florida, then I had to surf. It wasn't an option. It was something I had to do. When I say it's something I had to do, I don't mean that I had to force myself. If I could, I would surf every day the rest of my life, especially if it weren't for a responsibility I have to this thing called a job. When I say I must surf, I'm saying that when my love for surfing and my proximity to the beach combined, my mind and body required me to go. If I didn't go, I had to endure the pangs caused by this urge deep down inside of me that could only be calmed by at least a few hours catching some waves. The longer it took me to get back the beach the more persistent and undeniable the urge became, until it was all I could think about. It was almost like the waves knew that I had just moved within a few miles, and they were constantly beckoning for my attention. Living so close and loving to surf so much, my only option was to go.

Caring for the earth is the same way, taking action is a must. It isn't an option; it's something we have to do. I'm not talking about a must in terms of a nasty chore God asks us to do as a way to punish us or a good work required of us to get into heaven. It's not like that at all. Instead, taking action is a natural urge that comes to us in the process of being restored into the image of God. It's part of being made perfect. God's love enters our heart and removes the numbness caused by sin, which enables us to feel the pangs of the world around us. When our love for God and proximity to a damaged earth are brought together, the only thing that makes sense is to take action. When God's love begins to take up all the spaces of our hearts, the only option is to go and care for creation. As long as you allow God to shape you into perfection, there's no way for you to suppress the desire to take action by caring for creation.

Every day, there was a new wave for me to ride. Other than on days where the waves were so small a mouse couldn't surf it, I didn't have a problem exhausting my need to surf. If I had to surf, then all I needed to do was go. Every day, there is a pain in creation for us to heal. Unlike the occasional circumstances of an ocean with no waves, there really are no exceptions. For creation, every day brings abuse and mistreatment. If we must take action, then all we need to do is go.

SECTION TWO
OUR
QUIVER

When I say "quiver," I'm not talking about a pouch to carry arrows. I guess in a way it refers to a collection of weaponry, but in this case the arsenal isn't deadly. The arsenal pulled out of the quiver I'm talking about isn't used to inflict pain, although it does at times. Instead, its purpose is to do the opposite, which is to add joy to one's life. A true sign of a seasoned surfer is a diversified quiver.

A quiver is a surfer's collection of surfboards, and yes, I meant to use the plural. Almost every serious surfer owns several surfboards of different shapes and sizes. Even if it means giving up steak and eating peanut butter and jelly for every meal, someone sold out to surfing the best waves in any condition will do whatever it takes to buy the boards to make it happen. I don't think one board qualifies as a quiver, but a normal quiver could include anywhere from three to ten boards. I agree, ten is a bit excessive, but owners have reasons to justify the number of boards they own.

The reason for owning a quiver of boards is to own a board for every condition. The ocean isn't like other sports playing with fields; it's never the same. Every day and every place you surf produces a totally different wave, which requires an entirely different board. If you want to be prepared to surf in any condition, then you need to own the right boards to handle every wave type. For example, on a day when the waves are small and weak, it is better to ride a long board in order to catch more waves with longer rides. However, on a day when the waves are big and powerful, it is better to ride a short board in order to maximize speed and maneuverability. As the wave type becomes more specific, so do the characteristics of the board you need. The bigger and more diverse a surfer's quiver, the greater the potential to surf any day anywhere.

I'm sad to admit it, but my collection of two boards barely qualifies me to call it a quiver. For almost three years, I only owned one board. My first board is called a funshape. It is seven feet eight inches long, which is somewhere between a short board and a long board. A short board is generally around six feet long, and a long board is somewhere closer to nine feet in length. The design is meant to give a little of the best of both worlds, which means it paddles somewhat like a long board and turns somewhat like a short board. Because it functions like both, a funshape board adapts more easily to different wave conditions.

I say it adapts more easily, but not necessarily perfectly. There was at least one wave condition that brought out the worst in my funshape and me. It took me several experiences of walking away from the ocean feeling beat-up and frustrated to realize certain types of waves were not meant to be ridden on a funshape—at least not by me and my funshape. It was the type of day when the waves were big, plenty, and breaking way offshore. On days like this, the ocean looked like it was sending forth rows and rows of white water as far left and right as I could see. The only way to get to the rideable waves was to pass through several steep, thick walls of white water. A short board is light enough to duck under the wave, and a long board is buoyant enough to paddle quickly through the small openings between the crashing waves. A funshape doesn't have enough of either, which means the white and me went head to head. I would paddle as fast and hard as I could straight into the wall of water hoping to break through, almost like a torpedo. Sometimes I would make it through to the other side, and sometimes the wave would wash me back to where I started. After feeling like a rag doll being tossed around in a washing machine, I finally realized I couldn't make it all the way out. I just didn't have the right board to make it worth it. My quiver, or lack thereof, couldn't support me in all the different wave conditions.

Up to this point, I've challenged you to imagine a new understanding of holiness that includes caring for creation or the environment. Having determined the ultimate goal of the Christian life to be perfection, I've defined "Environmental Holiness" as God making us into new creations who reflect the image of God in our ability and responsibility to actively care for creation, but I haven't given you much to put in your quiver.

It's not fair for me to ask you to consider a vision of the Christian life that includes caring for creation if I'm not willing to provide support to back it up. To stop here and not go any further is like asking you to go surfing without giving you a board; it doesn't really make much sense. Without a board, you have nothing to support you. Actually, it wouldn't even be enough for me to give you one board; I'd need to stock your quiver with a variety of boards so you'd be prepared to surf any condition. I don't want to invite you into the water without giving you the right boards, because it'll only cause frustration to the point that you'll want to give up.

I want to help you start a quiver that is full of reasons supporting why caring for creation is part of the process of being shaped into the perfect image of God. God gives us a quiver full of reasons to help us understand why any of this makes sense or even matters to those of us who call ourselves Christians. It's not like when someone asks you to do something but won't give you a legitimate reason why. God doesn't do that to us. Through the Bible and our theology, God explains why we are called to take care of the earth and its environment. In the next few chapters, I will gather up a few of the reasons and explanations into one collection and offer the quiver to you. The good news is you don't have to eat peanut butter and jelly for the rest of your life to afford this quiver. It's free, so make some room.

CHAPTER 5
WAVE MAKER
DOCTRINE OF CREATION

The controversy is on-going: Should a true surfer support the construction of artificial surf parks? I'm sure most of you have been to a water park with a wave pool, which means you probably tried to either body surf the waves or let the waves do with you as it chooses while relaxing on an inner tube. It's an interesting sight to see hundreds of people bobbing up and down on the waves in a gigantic pool, some lying on yellow tubes while others doggy paddle for dear life. To be honest, I think wave pools are a lot of fun, but until recently I never thought it would be possible to surf in one.

As if the millions of miles of coastline aren't good enough for surfers, our world has decided it's time to design enormous pools specifically for surfing. Architects and engineers are working together to succeed in creating a pool that simulates the waves surfers experience in the ocean. Actually, such a pool has existed in Orlando for several years, but it is part of a water park that limits opportunities to surf for after hours. As I'm typing this, a water park solely for surfing is being built in Orlando, which will give central Florida's residents a second option.

Depending on where a person lives, a surfer may or may not be excited about the prospect of paying admission to surf near-perfect waves. For several of the surfers who've moved inland to pursue education or a better job or live closer to family, it's exciting to hear of the potential to surf again without moving back to the coast. A surf park may charge to ride their waves, but spending money on waves you know will be pumping definitely beats taking a vacation to the beach where there's never a guarantee the waves will be rideable. For those who live near the beach, it's insulting to even think about wasting money on phony waves. A surf park takes away from the challenge of adjusting to the always-changing conditions of the ocean, not to mention the physical prowess and skill it takes to paddle through rough waters. Surfers are on both sides of the issue, some give two thumbs up to surf parks, while the others turn up their noses at the idea.

When we remove all the trash-talking and whining on both sides of the debate, it all comes down to one main issue: What is producing the waves? It's a difference between being sold out to the natural production of waves in our earth's seas, or buying into a commercialized version of machine-powered waves. It's kind of like the choice between enjoying a bike ride on a trail through the natural beauty of the outside world or sitting on a bike at your local fitness center staring at a screen simulating the real world. A person may walk out of the gym feeling like they just rode to the top of Pike's Peak, but in reality, they missed out on the opportunity to experience the beauty of nature. Surfers face a similar decision, nature or machine.

The surfers who've decided to stay with the waves of the ocean are making a huge statement about their relationship to nature. In their own way, these surfers are showing respect and appreciation to the natural, and sometimes unnatural, flow of the earth's oceans. These surfers are forever grateful to the ocean for all the moments waves have sent their way. If the ocean had never produced waves, no one would have had the imagination to even think of a building an artificial surf park. Without the ocean, surfing wouldn't even exist. So by protesting against machine powered waves, surfers are basically acknowledging the true source of their waves, the ocean. These surfers have grasped a powerful truth they are not willing to let go of, and that truth is this: the ocean is their wave maker.

When we encounter the very first words of the Bible, we learn a truth just as powerful: God is the creator of the earth. God is the originator of the air we breathe, the ground we walk on, the trees we climb, the water we drink, the fruit we eat, and the beauty we see. Everything good that exists was made by God. God is recognized and affirmed as the creator of all things by the earliest writings of the Old Testament, by the writers of the New Testament, by the early creeds and councils, and by hymns and worship songs ever since. We can trace an emphasis on identifying God as Creator all the way back to Adam and Eve. Like the surfers who acknowledge what makes their waves, followers of Christ have remembered the work of their God as Creator.

It's not difficult to flip to Genesis 1 and 2 to read about the story of God creating the earth and all its inhabitants. For one who believes the truth of the Bible, it's nearly impossible to read the story contained in these two chapters and deny that God is the creator of everything. It's a bit more of a cumbersome task to discover references to God as Creator in the rest of the Old Testament, but once you start looking for them, you'll start seeing them everywhere. Here are a few examples:

"To the LORD your God belong the heaven and the highest heavens, the earth and all that is in it" (Deut. 10:14).

"You alone are the LORD. You made the heavens, the heaven of heavens with all their host, the earth and all that is on it, the seas and all that is in them. You give life to all of them, and the heavenly host bows down before You" (Neh. 9:6).

"The earth is the LORD'S, and all it contains, the world, and those who dwell in it" (Ps. 24:1).

"Who has measured the waters in the hollow of his hand, and marked off the heavens by the span, and calculated the dust of the earth by the measure, and weighed the mountains in a balance and the hills in a pair of scales? . . . Lift up your eyes on high and see who created these stars, the One who leads forth their host by number, He calls them all by name" (Isa. 40:12, 26a).

A core belief for God's people from the beginning of time is that God is our Creator. To be part of the people of God in the Old Testament meant affirming God as Creator.

There's a good chance that you've read the story in Genesis about God creating the earth and might be wondering what the New Testament has to say.

"The God who made the world and all things in it, since He is Lord of heaven and earth, does not dwell in temples made with hands; nor is he served by human hands, as though he needed anything, since he himself gives to all people life and breath and all things. And He made from one man every nation of mankind to live on all the face of the earth, having determined their appointed times and the boundaries of their habitation" (Acts 17:24-26).

"He said with a loud voice, 'Fear God and give him glory, because the hour of his judgment has come; worship him who made heaven and the earth and sea and the springs of waters'" (Rev. 14:7).

"For by Him all things were created, both in the heavens and on earth" (Col. 1:16a).

"Worthy are You, our Lord and God, to receive glory and honor and power, for you created all things, and because of your will they existed, and were created" (Rev. 4:11).

The New Testament writers do not skip a beat. The story of God's people who worship God as Creator isn't erased or forgotten by the followers of Christ in the New Testament. Remembering and worshipping God as Creator wasn't relegated to old school thinking and stored in the archives of ancient beliefs. Instead, those who followed Christ protected it as an essential part of their identity. Actually, they recognized that Jesus was part of the creative process. John 1:1-3 says, "In the beginning was the Word (Jesus), and the Word was with God, and the Word was God. He was in the beginning with God. All things came into being through Him; and apart from him nothing came into being that has come into being." Followers of Christ in the days of the New Testament affirmed the belief in God as Creator.

An emphasis on the belief that God is our Creator didn't stop with the New Testament, it was written into the creeds of the Early Church. The purpose of creeds is to make clear exactly what it is that Christians believe so as to protect it against any false teaching. Two ancient creeds in the Christian church that are still recognized, memorized, and repeated in many of our churches today are the Apostle's Creed and the Nicene Creed. The Apostle's Creed served to unify early believers who considered themselves followers of the way of Christ. Every ancient Christian who heard it spoken or were fortunate enough to read it with their own eyes affirmed the beginning statement: "I believe in God, the Father Almighty, the Creator of heaven and earth." The Nicene Creed was written and promoted by a council of religious leaders in the ancient city of Nicaea in the year A.D. 325. This creed begins with an almost identical statement: "We believe in one God the Father Almighty, Maker of heaven and earth, and of all things visible and invisible." The early creeds are the closest thing that Christianity has to a summary statement of the truths we believe in, and both begin with by giving a shout out to God as our Creator.

The importance of belief in God as Creator isn't limited to arguments about the origin of things, but it makes a difference in the way we live from day to day as well. God was recognized as Creator of all things in Genesis, in the New Testament, and in the Apostle's and Nicene Creeds. This belief influenced how Christians chose to walk on this earth. It is a belief that adjusts how a person uses the things of this earth, or at least causes you to pause and consider how your actions might affect what God has created. If God is the Creator of all things and created them to be good, then our responsibility as persons who are being made to reflect the image of God is to do everything we can to care for the earth by preserving and restoring its goodness.

Christianity believes God is the Creator of all things, and the rest of creation is crying out for us to understand how it makes a difference in our actions toward them. It's not a new thought, but maybe one that's been forgotten in the wake of new technology and first-world developments. Like a surf park, our culture offers us new ways to experience life that are simple and non-burdensome, but cause us to turn away from the goodness of our Creator. The lure of a life made easy invites us to choose a way of living that is artificial and fake, which neglects our responsibility to care for what God has created. For those who are being shaped into the image of God, a different story is being told. The belief that God is Creator of all things isn't just some relic stored away in a dusty attic only to be pulled out when it's time to make an argument against evolution. Everywhere they go, they carry with them the awareness that God is the one true Creator of all things, never to be forgotten. Whenever they are amazed by the beauty and wonder of the earth, their thoughts turn to God. As they remember God is the Creator of everything, they also remember their responsibility to protect and care for what God has created to be good. Like surfers who are committed to the ocean because it is the creator of waves, Christians who reflect the image of God are committed to caring for creation because God is Creator.

CHAPTER 6
CLARK FOAM SHUT-DOWN
ORIGINAL SIN

I have nightmares about surfboards. Go ahead and laugh, but it's true. No, the surfboards don't grow arms and legs and chase after me, although that would be cool. My nightmares are basically where I come face to face with the horror of my surfboard being dented, dinged, scratched, and even broken. Bad dreams shouldn't have this effect on me, but every time I have these dreams, I wake up depressed. For the first few minutes after waking, I have difficulty distinguishing reality versus my dream. In the initial moments of recovering from my dream-world, I believe that my board is actually broken. Unwanted emotions flood my heart and mind until I finally realize it was only a dream. My worst nightmare didn't come true, and my boards are safe.

Although nothing close to the horror of my nightmares, I remember the first time my board suffered a serious injury. My first board was an unexpected anniversary present from Brooklyn, which added a special significance to this treasured possession. It was custom-shaped according to my dimensions, plus Brooklyn personally chose the artwork for the top of the board. Upon receiving it as a gift, it became my baby.

I don't know if you've ever owned anything you were reluctant to share with others, but that's exactly how I felt with my board. I didn't even like people walking too close to it in my house for the fear that they would knock it over. If it was difficult for me to let anyone touch the board in my house, then you probably can imagine how hesitant I would be to let someone ride it. Well, I found myself in that very situation. I invited a friend to go surfing with me who had never surfed before and didn't have his own board. Since I was the one who wanted him to try surfing, I had to let down my selfishness and allow him to use my board. For the first time since owning the board, I let someone else try it out.

The ocean is huge and contains miles and miles of beach, so I thought we were far enough away from any potential problems. I intentionally made sure the closest surfer was out of harm's way—so I thought. I'm not sure how it happened, but my friend was riding a wave like a boogie board, and from out of nowhere, a long boarder intersected his path and smacked right into the side of my board. It was like an SUV crashing into the side of a mid-sized car; my board received all of the damage. This was the first time I let someone use my board; and it gets a huge ding in the side.

I didn't know much about surfboard technology, but I knew my board couldn't survive with a gaping hole in its side. I took it to a local surf shop, and they explained the problem. On the inside of most surfboards is a foam core that can't be repaired or replaced. Luckily, water hadn't made its way to the foam in my board, which means they were able to patch the ding and make it like new again. I walked away from the shop with a cosmetically altered board and a new appreciation for foam. Little did I know how important foam was to the surf world.

The news was plastered all over the front of my latest surf magazine: Clark Foam—the world's leading supplier of foam blanks used in surfboards—had unexpectedly shut down for good. Ironically, at least for an industry that holds a special respect for the ocean, the issue leading to the closure of Clark Foam was environmental violations.

The announcement that Clark Foam was shutting down sent shockwaves throughout the world of surfing, and those feeling it most were shapers who made a living making boards with a foam core. One internationally recognized shaper commented on the news: "This is going to affect everyone. It's pretty hard to make a surfboard without a blank, and these big labels are doing over a thousand a month. I can't believe this news. Are you sure it's real? You're not joking?"[1]

Unfortunately, the messiness of it all wasn't contained within the limits of Clark Foam. Losing 90% of the world's foam severely disrupted the production of surfboards, and for some shapers it meant closing the doors to their own shops. According to the logic of supply and demand, the shortage of foam led to an unexpected increase in the price of boards, thus affecting the pocketbook of surfers. With no foam and little hope of Clark Foam's return, shapers scurried to find new technology and alternative sources for surfboard blanks. In short, the consequences of the mistakes leading to the Clark Foam shutdown were passed on to the rest of the surfing world.

The effects of Clark Foam's owner, Gordon "Grubby" Clark, to turn away from a commitment to the environment was felt by the majority of the surfing world and may easily be understood as surfing's "Original Sin." That is: *the consequence of the mistake of one person has been passed on to every person who owns a board, every shaper who plans to make another board, and every shop who hopes to sell another board.* The effects of Clark Foam's sin has stung the surfing world and left it to recover from a mess that will take who knows how much time, money, and imagination to overcome. Surfers and shapers everywhere have inherited the consequences of Clark Foam's neglect of the environment, and now they must do everything they can to repair the damages.

If you've ever read the Book of Genesis or heard the story of Adam and Eve, then the story of Clark Foam might sound familiar. The event of Adam and Eve using their free choice to neglect God's command to avoid eating the fruit on one tree (Gen. 2:15-17) has affected all of humanity and creation (Gen. 3). *From one act of sin, everything God made perfect is now stained and blemished with imperfections.* When we read Genesis 1 and 2, we learn that God created everything; and it was good, including man and woman (Gen. 1:3, 1:10, 1:12, 1:18, 1:21, 1:25, and 1:31). As we learned in an earlier chapter, humans were created a little higher than the rest of creation; they were made in the image of God. In the beginning, everything was good and perfect until one sin slithered into the story and changed the rest of history. The moment Adam and Eve decided to disobey God and touched their lips to the forbidden fruit, sin invaded our world and stained it with a mess that every succeeding generation has been left to clean up.

The name given to the act Adam and Eve committed is "Original Sin," because that's exactly what it was, the first act of disobedience against God's will. It's also called "original" because it is the one act that enabled sin to influence every human in history to have an inclination to follow selfish and evil desires. We can trace every sinful thought and action back to Adam and Eve's original sin. Without their one sin, our thoughts and actions would be perfect. I'm stunned to realize that one act of disobedience has created a mess to be cleaned up by every person who has been and will ever be born on this earth. "Original Sin" affects all of us.

John Wesley, a preacher and theologian in the 18th century, wrote a sermon alerting others of the tragedy of Original Sin. He said "that by one man's disobedience all men were constituted sinners; that in 'Adam all died', spiritually died, lost the life and the image of God; that fallen, sinful Adam then 'begat a son in his own likeness.'"[2] Did you catch that? Because of Adam's sin, we've lost the image of God we were created to reflect. God created humanity to be good and perfect, but Adam's sin has distorted what God created us to be. Wesley makes it clear by referencing Genesis 6:5, "then the LORD saw that wickedness of man was great on the earth, and that every intent of the thoughts of his heart was only evil continually." Because of Original Sin, we've lost our natural ability to know God's will, which means we're definitely not living up to our responsibility to always follow what God would have us do. Wesley puts it another way: "we bring with us into the world a corrupt, sinful nature. . .That hereby we are prone to all that is evil, and adverse from all that is good; that we are full of pride, self-will, unruly passions, foolish desires."[3]

However, the effect of Original Sin doesn't stop with humanity, at least not according to John Wesley's understanding of God's Word. In a different sermon, he mentions how remarkable it is to consider how the universe was organized by God into a perfect system. It's remarkable because God created the universe and everything in it to be intimately connected to every other part in a way that functions without fault. Not only is Wesley amazed by the beauty of the intricacies of the universe when God created it, but he also believes it's the duty of every believer to seek to understand how creation was before it was "disordered and depraved in consequence of the sin of man."[4] Whoa, wait a minute! Is he saying that Adam's sin not only messed up the image of God in us, but it also had an affect on the rest of creation? Wesley goes on to say that with sin, Adam "threw not only himself but likewise the whole creation, which was intimately connected with him, into disorder, misery, [and] death."[5] Everything God created, both human and non-human, has been affected by the disease of Original Sin. If God created all the parts of the universe in connection with each other, then it's impossible for any part not to experience the painful effects of Adam and Eve's one mistake.

As disturbing as it must have been for thousands of surfboard shapers to learn of the effects Clark Foam's mistakes would have on their lives, it's more disturbing to learn of the effects of Adam's and Eve's sin on all of creation. Left alone, an understanding of Original Sin wreaks hopelessness. The story of God's work in creation, however, doesn't end in Genesis. God doesn't leave us for dead, but "the great Physician of souls applies medicine to heal this sickness; to restore human nature, totally corrupted in all its faculties."[6] Jesus lived on this earth, died on a cross, conquered death, and rose again in order to be the healing balm that can restore us into the image of God. Wesley ends his sermon, "you know that the great end of religion is to renew our hearts in the image of God, to repair that total loss of righteousness and true holiness which we sustained by the sin of our first parent. You know that all religion which does not answer this end, all that stops short of this, the renewal of our soul in the image of God, after the likeness of him that created it, is no other than a poor farce and a mere mockery of God, to the destruction of our own soul."[7]

The Bible is a story of tragedy as humanity loses the image of God through Adam and Eve's sin, but it is also a story of redemption as all of us have a chance to have the image of God restored through Jesus' victory over sin. The story of salvation is about God doing everything possible, including dying on a cross, to undo the mistake of Original Sin by restoring the image of God in humanity. God wants to include you in the new story that is being written, a story where you regain the image of God and all of creation returns to the goodness it was created to be. God has promised to erase the affects of Original Sin, and we can be a part of it if we allow Him to re-shape us into the persons who reflect His likeness.

How does Original Sin and God restoring His image in us relate to creation, the earth, or the environment? Keep in mind that Original Sin not only affected humanity, but it also messed up the goodness of all creation. God created everything in connection with all the other parts, which means when one part isn't working correctly, the whole system is thrown out of whack. When the image of God in humanity was damaged by Original Sin, everything else in creation followed suit. It's kind of like a trickle-down effect: sin trickled down from humanity and infected the goodness and perfection of the rest of creation. The earth suffers from humanity's loss of the image of God.

God's purpose in making us perfect by reshaping us into the image of God isn't just about us, but it's about redeeming all of creation. They go hand in hand. You can't have one without the other. As God begins to restore us, we begin to think and act like the persons we were created to be in the beginning. We become conscious of the responsibility given to us in Genesis 1:26-30 to care for all the plants, the animals on land, the fish in the sea, the birds of the air, and everything else that makes up earth. Once again, we realize that we are only a single part of a once-perfect system, where our actions affect the well-being of all the other parts of the universe. As more and more of Original Sin is replaced with the image of God, we begin to understand the goodness of the universe as it was created and we do all that we can to adjust our lifestyle to heal rather than hurt the earth. As God restores the damage of Original Sin in us, God is also restoring the damage done to the rest of creation through us.

Caring for creation isn't something we have to do as Christians; it's something we will do naturally as people who reflect the image of God. To ask God to save you from the bondage of sin, or Original Sin, is the same as asking God to reshape you into a person made in the likeness of God. If God is truly able to restore God's image in you, then it's inevitable that you will do whatever it takes to care for the earth. It's a difficult task to reflect God and neglect caring for creation. God made everything good, so to be like God means to restore the earth, animals, and the environment to goodness. God's in the process of reversing the affects of Original Sin and desires to include all of us in on the project.

I'm positive the surf world will recover from the shutdown of Clark Foam. In three short years, great strides have already been made. I'm even more certain that humanity and the rest of creation will recover from the mistake of Adam and Eve. God has been and will continue to redeem the world from the effects of Original Sin until the day when Christ returns and makes all things new. God wants to restore the image of God in you and through you to restore the goodness of creation.

CHAPTER 7
CRUISE LINES
LOVE OF GOD
AND NEIGHBOR

What happens when you are swimming and suddenly feel the urge to relieve your body of the three cans of soda you drank? Every time I feel nature calling me while swimming in a pool, the first thing that comes to mind is my dad's voice saying, "If you go in the pool, it will turn red." I know my dad was only trying to scare me, but even to this day, I'm hesitant to treat the pool as a toilet for the fear that it may be the one pool that uses the magical dye. Hopefully, you have a better reason to "hold it" than a fear of being embarrassed by red dye, but I'm guessing a lot of you are just like me.

Now place me in a lake or the ocean, and it's a different story. I don't know if I feel more free because I'm in nature and it's a natural act, but all my fears dissipate when I'm in the ocean. Maybe because the ocean is so big my mind tells me it can't really make a difference, or maybe I feel okay about it because the fish are doing the same thing, so why shouldn't I join them? Maybe I don't feel guilty because I know there's no way anyone would ever find out.

However, my thought processes change as soon as I put on a wetsuit. There's only one reason to wear a wetsuit—cold weather. A wetsuit day for me means extending my time in the water as long as I can, which increases my sessions by about two or three hours. To make putting on a wetsuit and enduring the cold worth it, I do everything I can to stay in the water as long as possible. You can probably imagine what happens after being in the water for three or four hours—nature begins to call. It's a long paddle back to shore. Besides, once I'm out of the water, surfing is over for the day. What a dilemma. Now my perspective begins to change. It's not an easy decision to fill up a wetsuit with whatever fluids my body wants to get rid of, especially considering wetsuits are made to keep liquid from passing through its material. I guess it could warm me up, but it could be with me for a few hours. All of a sudden, I don't feel so free in the ocean, because now it's all about me. Kind of sad, don't you think? The only time I'm willing to hold back is when it affects me in a bad way.

If you've been grossed out by my discussion of bodily functions so far, then you may want to skip past this next section. Why? Because what I just talked about is nothing compared to the thousands and possibly millions of gallons of waste dumped into the earth's oceans every day. If you've ever swum in the ocean, there's a good chance you were less than 3 miles from the location it was dumped. Until a couple years ago, I didn't realize this either.

A friend of mine told me he might be participating in a protest, "Pump Don't Dump," at the cruise port with a group of surfers in the area. A local chapter from the Surfrider Foundation organized a paddle-out for any surfer interested in making a statement to the cruise lines who use the ocean's waters as the place to dump their waste at the detriment of sea life and the rest of the ocean's environment. The plan was to paddle out toward the cruise ships on their surfboards in a group large enough to be noticed and loud enough to be heard. My friend didn't make it that day, but the issue was important enough to rally the efforts of several surfers from all walks of life who were willing to use their day off as a time to fight for the ocean.

I had no idea of the pollution that can be caused by cruise ships. If you've ever seen a cruise ship or been on one, then you've most likely realized the enormity of their size. Some of the ships are so big you could probably combine the populations from two or three small towns and still have room for more guests. They are like mini-towns floating on the ocean, and they have the pollution problems to prove it. Actually, if you were to compare the pollution from a cruise ship to the pollution from a city with the same population, you would find that the ship's pollution is worse per capita.[8] Crazy, huh?

Here's the amount of waste produced by an average-sized cruise ship (about 3,000 passengers) on a typical one-week voyage:

- 1 million gallons of "gray water" (waste from sinks, showers, laundries and galleys).
- 210,000 gallons of sewage from toilets.
- 25,000 gallons of oily bilge water.
- Over 100 gallons of hazardous or toxic waste (which includes per-

chloroethylene from dry-cleaning, photo-processing wastes, paint waste, solvents, print shop wastes, fluorescent light bulbs, and batteries).

- 50 tons of garbage and solid waste (plastic, paper, wood, cardboard, food waste, cans, and glass).

- Diesel exhaust emissions equivalent to thousands of automobiles.[9]

As if these pollutants weren't enough, cruise ships also pose a threat to the earth's ocean with what is referred to as "ballast water." Ballast water is seawater pumped into the hull of the ship to ensure stability.[10] Typically, ballast water is taken in at one port and then released at another port, which threatens the waters with invasive species and diseases transported from the original port to the other.

Certain regulations have been placed on cruise ships to prevent widespread dumping into our planet's lakes, rivers, and oceans. Here's a list of the regulations:

- Cruise ships (and other ships) are required to have "marine sanitation devices", which are designed to prevent the discharge of untreated sewage. Sewage must be treated to specified standards before discharge if the ship is stationary or if it is within a specified distance (generally three miles) of shore. When the ship is beyond three miles from shore, there are no restrictions on the release of untreated sewage.

- There are no restrictions on the release of gray water, except in the Great Lakes.

- Discharge of oil or oily water into US navigable waters, adjoining shorelines or waters which may affect natural resources within 200 miles of shore is prohibited, unless the oily water is passed through an oil-water separator designed to reduce the oil concentration to 15 parts per million (ppm) within 12 miles of shore or within 100 ppm beyond 12 miles from shore.

- Hazardous wastes should be properly packaged and labeled and disposed in permitted on-shore facilities, but the applicability of the Resource Conservation and Recovery Act (RCRA) to ships and Cruise Lines is not clear.

- The dumping of garbage at sea is prohibited within certain distances from shore, generally ranging from 3 to 25 miles. Dumping of plastic is prohibited everywhere at sea, and all discharge or incineration of garbage must be recorded in a Garbage Record Book.

- Although there are pending new rules from the EPA on diesel engine emissions, there are essentially no present emission restrictions and the proposed new rules are still much weaker than for land-based emission sources.[11]

Cruise lines have confirmed the old saying, "laws are meant to be broken." As the records show, the cruise line industry has had difficulty complying with the existing weak regulations. Over a six-year period from 1993 to 1998, several cruise ships were involved in 87 separate cases of illegal discharges into US waters, some of which included multiple incidents of illegal dumping that numbered in the hundreds.[12] One cruise line was penalized an amount of 33.5 million dollars to settle dumping complaints that occurred between 1994 and 1998. The technology exists to prevent or at least cut back on cruise line pollution, but until effective regulations are enforced, the list of violations will continue to grow more and more each year.

For those of you who don't live near the coast, maybe this doesn't seem like a big deal. For those of us who live in coastal states, however, the problem is right next door. It's kind of weird to think of a moving vessel this way, but a cruise ship is actually our neighbor. On the days they're not out to sea working, the ship or ships are parked in our neighborhood. On certain days of the week, we're greeted by towering ships the size of a small town as we crest the top of a bridge on the minutemen causeway leading straight to the beach. Unlike other neighbors, cruise ships entertain thousands of guests at the same time, sometimes dropping off and picking up new passengers once or twice a week. As if one cruise liner isn't enough, we're neighbors to eight different ships. This means we share our waterways with about thirty to forty thousand people a week. Can you imagine that many people moving in and out of your neighborhood on a weekly basis?

I don't want to sound like a downer on cruise lines, because I've had worse neighbors living in the house next to me or the apartment above me. The problem with cruise lines is the same problem I've experienced with other neighbors who do whatever they want regardless of how it affects others. Some neighbors invite 30 teenagers over to their houses to party hard and loud until the wee hours of the morning. Some vacuum the carpet, run the washing machine, and walk in high heel shoes in the top floor apartment at 11:00 P.M. Then there are those who dump thousands of gallons of untreated sewage into the earth's ocean waters when there's technology to prevent it. They are neighbors who aren't really neighbors at all, because they act like no one else exists.

I know when I think about neighbors who live recklessly at others expense, I've always thought to myself, "that's not me." I'm confident that I don't throw parties at my house, I'm not loud at night, and I don't dump my sewage into the ocean, at least as far as I know. Yet one day God challenged me with these questions: "What are you doing to care for my creation?" and "How does it affect your neighbor?" Up to this point in my life, I knew there were some things I needed to work on to better love my neighbor, but I thought I was doing pretty well. Yet, God had to throw in the whole thing about taking care of creation as a way to be a good neighbor. If you throw in my irresponsibility toward creation, I'm not much better than the cruise ship that dumps raw sewage into clean waters.

Like so many other times in the Gospels, Jesus was put to the test in the story of the Good Samaritan found in the Book of Luke (Luke 10:25-37). A lawyer stepped forward to ask Jesus a leading question, "Teacher, what shall I do to inherit eternal life?" Jesus answered him, "You shall love the Lord your God with all your heart, and with all your soul, and with all your strength, and with all your mind; And your neighbor as yourself." From this story, we discover that the love of God and the love of neighbors can't be separated. To love God means to love our neighbor—which means everything else we do is wrapped up in this simple command given by Jesus.

John Wesley said in his sermon "On Love," "If I give all possessions to feed the poor, and if I deliver my body to be burned, but do not have love, it profits me nothing."[13] Wesley used 1 Corinthians 13:3 as his Bible text for one simple reason, to convince the audience that love is essential to being a Christian. Without love, Wesley believed a person could not enter into eternal life. Love is serious stuff.

Wesley couldn't write a sermon called "On Love" and give it so much weight in matters of eternity without defining what love is. It's really no surprise that he quickly turns to the great commandment spoken by Jesus, which is to love God and neighbor. He's not satisfied to merely mention loving God and neighbor, but he proceeds to define both forms of love. The first part of his discussion on love comes as no surprise; the word "neighbor" refers to our fellow human beings. However, he doesn't stop there. Surprisingly, he invites us to stretch our definition of the word "neighbor" to include God's creatures. I'm not talking about creepy crawlies that live under your bed. Instead of limiting God's command to love our neighbor, Wesley challenges us to understand that it also means to "love many of his (God's) creatures in the strictest sense—to delight in them, to enjoy them."[14] It's hard enough to love our own family; now we discover we must love creatures too. Can we at least start with our pets?

God requires us to love our neighbor, including the creatures. According to Wesley, any person who realizes the importance of this command "feels an ardent and uninterrupted thirst after the happiness of all his fellow-creatures. So that whether he thinks or speaks, or whatever he does, it all points to the same end—the advancing, by every possible way, the happiness of all his fellow creatures."[15] As the image of God is restored in us, love fills up our heart and removes the residue of original sin, and we begin to love our neighbor without strain or struggle. Our thoughts and actions confirm God's love for all creatures, both human and non-human.

So far I've picked on cruise lines, but what about everyone else? What is the rest of the world doing to care for creation as a way to love our neighbor? There's an inseparable link between how we treat the environment and the well-being of other human beings and earthly creatures. Poor care of the earth leads to lower life expectancy, serious illnesses, diseases, and death for many people who weren't a part of the exploitation of God's creation. They just happen to live in a place that receives the runoff effect of others' irresponsible behavior, while those responsible for the pollution enjoy life unaware or unconcerned. Sometimes, abuse of the environment is due to ignorance, and sometimes it's premeditated. Regardless of one's intention, it is still detrimental to the well-being of our neighbors.

All over the world, God's creatures have suffered and even died as a result of others' negligence toward the care of creation. The earth and the environment are abused at the expense of others. Creation and its inhabitants are hurting, yet there are those who walk on by like the problem doesn't exist. The Good Samaritan story ends in Luke 10:37 with Jesus' words, "Go and do likewise." Love your neighbors, both humans and creatures, by taking care of creation.

Hopefully you haven't forgotten already that—as Christians—we are searching for perfection. Our hope is that God would make us perfect by restoring in us the perfect image of God. There's no better way to summarize what perfection—it is love. "The first branch of it is the love of God: And as he that loves God loves his brother also, it is inseparably connected with the second: 'Thou shalt love thy neighbour as thyself.'"[16]

CHAPTER 8
PICKING UP TRASH
ACTS OF MERCY

Going to the beach can be a fiasco, especially when you're married to a youth pastor. When an entire youth group is invited to go to the beach, a simple day easily turns into a family reunion-type event. A week or so ahead of time, Brooklyn announces when we were planning to meet and at what particular beach location we would set up camp for the day. When I say "set up camp," I'm not exaggerating. Believe it or not, some of the teenagers who live in Florida don't spend much time in the sun. Actually, some of them prefer to wear jeans and sweatshirts all year long, so their arms and legs are rarely exposed to the sun. When they shed full-body coverings for swimwear, sunburn becomes an immediate issue. I'm talking about teenagers who somehow find a way to forget to apply sunscreen. I don't know, maybe it's not cool to wear sunscreen or it's a way to rebel against their parents; somehow, sunscreen doesn't find its way onto their skin. We're forced to literally set up a huge canopy-like tent right on the beach for those students who need a break from the sun's damaging rays—not a camping tent, but an open-air tent, a big blue canvas roof with no walls and four poles sticking out of the sand. If the poles weren't forged deep enough in the sand, the wind would pick the whole thing up and carry it down the beach. When all was said and done, it took us about an hour to set up camp.

A few hours at the beach just isn't enough time. It was called a beach day not a beach hour, so we spent all day at the beach, from early morning to late afternoon. The students definitely packed like they were planning to be there all day, some of them were even prepared to stay a couple days. They packed food, candy, drinks, games, balls, clothes, towels, cell-phones, and whatever else would fit in a backpack. As if they didn't have enough junk food to hold them over until dinner, a few pizzas were ordered to share while lounging under the tent. Our little camp on the beach could easily be compared to a cabin or dorm room at church camp. Each student had their designated area to pile all their junk. Stuff was lying everywhere and strongly resembled a shipwreck.

It's amazing how much trash was created in one day by twenty to thirty middle school and high school students. Within a few hours, a nice clean spot on the beach was littered with potato chip bags, candy wrappers, plastic bottles, pieces of clothing, beach towels, beach toys, and the occasional flip-flop sandal. Evidence would suggest that the students' backpacks were definitely lighter by the end of the day. Needless to say, tearing down camp didn't hold as much excitement as setting up, because the majority of our time was spent cleaning up our mess.

If you can imagine the amount of trash created by twenty students, then multiply it by thousands and thousands and thousands to come up with the true quantity left behind every day. It's sad to consider how much trash humans produce at the beach each day and disappointing to realize how little of it is ever picked up. Beaches and oceans are some of the most beautiful places to visit on all of God's creation, and somehow the human tendency is to damage its sacredness with our trash. In a way, we treat sandy beaches like our own private, or maybe I should say public, litter-box.

To be completely honest, trash on the beach wasn't something in the front of my mind when I went surfing—that is until one of my surfing buddies altered my perspective. Meet Bill. There are a couple things you need to know about Bill. The first thing you should know is that he recently returned to surfing. He was a once a grom (grom is surf lingo for young surfer) on the east coast of Florida, where he surfed most of the spots I surf today. I can't give you the exact reason why, but there was a period in his life when he gave up surfing. A couple of years ago, he decided to give surfing a try once again. (I like to believe it was because of me, but that's not really true.) Now, nearly two years later, he owns a quiver of surfboards, checks the surf everyday after work, and has surfed in Costa Rica twice. It's official, Bill has a renewed love for surfing. The second thing you should know is that he's a committed Christian who's always seeking to grow in his relationship with God. Every time we talk, he tells me about something new God is challenging him to think, believe, or do. Bill is one of the rare people you come across in life who you know has an authentic relationship with God.

One day I am walking along doing my surf thing without any thought of beach trash, and Bill decides to spoil my ignorance. Spoil may be too harsh a word, so instead I'll say he opened my mind. I am not bitter; I promise I'm not. It's just that I had grown so comfortable with focusing all my attention on the waves that it shook me a little to be awakened to my own blindness. I was so self-absorbed with doing what I wanted to do that nothing else really mattered, not even the trash I had to step on or over to get to the waves.

The challenge from Bill came to me via e-mail. In the e-mail, he told me about a story of a teenager in California who came up with a plan to eliminate trash on the beach. The plan is simple: every time you go to the beach, pick up three pieces of trash more than what you came with, and dispose of them properly on your way out. If every person who visited the beach would follow this plan, eventually our beaches would be completely trash free. It doesn't get much easier than that, just three extra pieces of trash every time you leave the beach.

Bill took the teenager's plan to heart and made a commitment to make it a part of his surfing experience, and he challenged me to do same thing. Since receiving that e-mail, there hasn't been a time when I've surfed with Bill that he's left the beach without picking up at least three pieces of trash. Because of his faithfulness to do his part, my perspective on a day of surfing has changed. I'm no longer blind to the trash that litters the sand like a minefield; instead, I've made it a part of my experience to pick up three extra pieces of trash as well. It's such a simple act.

As simple as they may sometimes seem, our "acts" matter to God. I'm not just talking about praying, reading the Bible and going to church, though these are important. I'm referring to the conscious decisions we make everyday to do something with our head, hands, and feet to share the love of God. It may be taking care of someone who's sick, helping out someone who is poor, protecting someone who is weak, befriending someone who is lonely, or even caring for creation. Our "acts" include everything we give, speak, or do to promote the well-being of someone or some thing. Our "acts of mercy" matter to God because, through them, God's grace is given to us. When we're willing to step outside of our own self-centeredness and do something good for someone other than ourselves, God is even more ready to do something good in us by making us perfect. Every time we act out of love for something outside ourselves, God's love is active in our hearts, restoring us into His image. It's like there's a power-line running from God to us. Any time we dare to do good acts, the power-line receives an extra charge and races toward us to fill our love-meter to full-capacity. If only we'd dare more often.

It's a cyclical process that begins and ends with God. God acts first, loving us enough to do what we couldn't do for ourselves, which is to conquer sin by living a sinless life, dying on a cross, and defeating death by rising from the dead. God acts first. The moment we believe and trust what Jesus did for us, we become followers of Christ. As you already know, the greatest commandment summarizes what it means to follow the way of Christ by telling us to love God and our neighbors. "The love of God naturally leads to works of piety" including praying, reading the Bible, and sharing in the Lord's Supper, and "the love of neighbor naturally leads all that feel it to works of mercy."[17]

We act second. All of our actions begin to look totally different when we shift our focus from pleasing self to caring for the needs of others. The things we do and the way we do them are motivated by a concern for the well-being of our neighbors, including all of creation.

God acts last. None of our actions goes unnoticed by God. He recognizes the good works we've done and pours grace and love all over our hearts. For the second time, God does for us what we can't do for ourselves—make us into to persons who reflect the image of God. By acting last, He starts the whole process over again.

I know the next thing I'm about to say could very easily get me into trouble, but I'll say it anyway. When it comes down to it and you are forced to choose between doing your devotions, saying a prayer, and going to church OR loving your neighbor with acts of mercy, God prefers your acts of mercy. I'm not saying you should skip church every week to plant a new tree, although that wouldn't be a bad idea once in awhile. However, if in the crisis of a moment, we are forced to decide between reading our devotions or limiting the damages of an oil spill by assisting with emergency clean-up, God would be pleased for us to postpone devotions to relieve the stress of creation. Sounds crazy, I know, but imagine what the world would be like if we spent half as much time caring for creation as we did listening to a choir sing and a pastor preach. Both are good, but one of them tends to be neglected, and it's not listening in church. God desires balance, and you might even say He prefers acts of mercy.

Our acts of mercy toward creation are opportunities for God to move us closer and closer to the ultimate goal of perfection. Why would anyone choose anything else? When I think about this, I feel like a secret has been let out of the bag. For most of my life, I didn't have this perspective on doing good for others with my actions. It's no one person's fault, but I was caught up in a tug of war between the idea that you had to pray, read your Bible, and go to church to be a Christian versus the idea that doing good couldn't make you a Christian. On the one hand, I felt pressure to never skip prayer, devotions, and church. On the other hand, I felt like I needed to conceal some of my actions so people wouldn't think I was trying to get to heaven by good works. The cat has been let of the bag for me, because I now know those feelings were false. God's commandment to love our neighbor isn't a stumbling block, but a blessing. God asks us to love others, because every time we do, it's a new opportunity for God to shape who we are. Every time we love our neighbor, including creation, our hearts soften, and God is able to mold and shape it into love.

Bill challenged me to do a simple act: pick up three extra pieces of trash. Is it really so simple? If Bill and I are honest with ourselves, we probably need to admit that most of the world will never make a commitment to pick up beach trash. Seriously, we're only two people, three if you count the boy who came up with the idea. We could pick up 100 pieces of trash every time we surf and still not make a noticeable difference, so what's the point, right? The point is that every time we care for creation, God's hands go to work on our hearts, shaping them into the beautiful image of Christ. From this perspective, picking up three extra pieces of trash doesn't seem so simple. Actually, it's mind-blowing.

CHAPTER 9
MY HOME BREAK
STEWARDSHIP

There's a huge difference between locals and out-of-towners. I had no idea until we moved to the coast, which made all the dirty looks I received make more sense. For about the first year of surfing, I drove an hour from the east side of Orlando to whichever beach was most convenient. My surf skills weren't good enough to have a favorite spot, so the majority of the time, the deciding factor in which beach to surf was free parking. Sounds cheap, I know, but I was a graduate student hanging out with a few high school students, so our wallets were barely able to cover the gas. We had no idea we were invading local territory, which I'm sure was obvious by our surf etiquette.

Locals are surfers who actually live on the coast and are within at least a ten to fifteen minute drive from the beach. A local is someone who knows all the surf spots in their area, and by "know" I mean they understand which beach's waves break better at a certain time of day and under a certain type of ocean conditions. If it's high tide or low tide, they know where to go. If the wind is heavy, they know the beach to visit. If the wave size is small, they know where to go. If one spot doesn't look good, they know where else to go. Locals know every beach like the back of their hand.

Out-of-towners, at least from my experience, live inland, usually an hour or more from the coast. They might be knowledgeable of one or two surf spots, which means they've been there before and back a couple times since. If you pressure them, they might even be able to show you where they are on a map. Their expertise when it comes to which beach is best for what conditions is limited, if not non-existent. It's not that out-of-towners are dumb, but when they go to the beach, it's an all-day event. They get up early and stay late, and all the time in between is spent in the water. There's no time to dilly-dally around trying to figure out which beach will be best at what time or under how much wind speed. It's all about getting to the beach and in the water as fast as you can, which makes it nearly impossible to learn the ins and outs of every spot.

Locals may have their finger on the ups and downs of all the different beaches, but they also have their favorite spot. When the waves are good everywhere or all else fails, they end up at the same beach. It's what they might consider home, the place where most of their memories are made. It's not just somewhere to surf, but a place to hang out with friends and share the water with people they've at least seen before. As much as there's a family feel at a local's home break, a pecking order is also in place. Everybody knows the limits of their own skills and will place themselves in the line-up accordingly. It's a funny sight to look at the water and realize everyone has separated themselves into several small packs or clusters, each according to skill level. The top surfers place themselves in prime position to catch the best waves, while everyone else claims the next best position in descending order of ability. The least skilled surfers end up with the worst position, but it's no big deal, they're happy to be able to call this beach "home."

It's a privilege to call a beach your home break, because when it comes down to it, not everyone is welcome. There are miles and miles of coastline, but the waves don't break the same on every beach. It's a fact that some beaches break better than others, and like I said, locals are keenly aware of the ones that are better. Sadly, there's not enough space at the best spots for every local to surf at the same time, so the whole pecking order thing comes into play again. If a person wants to surf at the sickest (by sick I mean best) break in town, they need to earn that right with their ability to tear up the wave. An ordinary Joe or Jane off the street can't paddle out at the best spot and expect to be welcomed with open arms. If you can't surf as well as everyone else, then you're pretty much not welcome. If you're lucky, those who call the premiere breaks home will send you packing without a scratch on you or your board.

A surfer is basically homeless until they find the break to match their talent, or lack thereof. Until one finds a place to fit in, they might as well be considered an out-of-towner. Sure, they can jump from place to place every time they go out, but what does that look like to those who call it home? It looks a lot like an out-of-towner. No surfer who lives near the beach wants the appearance of someone from out of town, and so the pecking order naturally falls into place. Even if it's painful to be orphaned by the best breaks in town, it's still better to claim a home break that isn't as good in order to gain the status of a true "local." In the words of Dorothy from the Wizard of Oz, "There's no place like home," even if it's not the best gig in town.

I wish someone had given me a manual on all of this before I started surfing. If someone would have let me know about this whole "home break" complex, then I probably could have saved myself from a hearing a few four letter words followed by a certain finger pointed toward the sky. I didn't know I was invading sacred ground, crashing a family reunion in the water. When they screamed expletives in my direction or shot evil looks my way as they paddled by, I assumed they were talking to somebody else. I honestly didn't know they saw me as an out-of-towner. I guess the only thing that protected me from getting into a fight was my ignorance. I avoided a major confrontation because I didn't respond, and the main reason I didn't respond was because I didn't know they were talking to me. It's not unusual for surfers to defend their territory with a fist, but somehow I avoided a fight by the simple fact that I was unaware. For the longest time, I was the dreaded out-of-towner and didn't even know it.

Eventually, my status changed to a "local" when we moved closer to the coast and I found a beach to call home. Prior to moving to the east coast, I had about six months of surfing experience under my belt at 24 years old—not much to brag about, especially considering the majority of surfers have been on a board since they were old enough to walk. Needless to say, my home break was at the bottom of the totem pole, the least coveted of the better breaks in town. It didn't take long, however, before I felt confident enough to start searching for a new home with better waves. I wasn't content with being a bottom feeder; I wanted to move up in the surfing world of east central Florida, and so I did. I eventually found a better break to call home, Second Light. It's still far from the premiere spot, but at least it isn't the worst. Somehow, I gained the perspective of most of the other local surfers, that there aren't enough good waves for everyone to share.

For many local surfers, it's all about "me." Even though there are hundreds of miles of beaches, the word "share" is rarely used by a local. We had to earn the respect to surf at our home break, so we're not about to give our waves to just anybody. Our home break isn't like Disney World; we don't like crowds, and we're definitely not going to stand in line behind some stranger for an hour waiting our turn to ride the next wave. Every wave that crests the horizon is mine, and if not mine, then my buddy paddling next to me. I'm sure you've seen the t-shirt athletes sometimes wear that says, "There's no *I* in team." Well, you can pretty much throw that whole idea out the window, because there's no team spirit at our home breaks. We're a bunch of individuals chasing the same waves, and there are no hard feelings about anyone else's wave count. Sure, most of us are friends, and we'll have a good time while waiting on the next set of waves, but when the waves come, it's all about "me."

What a gloomy picture of local surfers, huh? I've made them out to be self-centered individuals who think the only thing that stands in the way of them and their happiness is you and everyone else in the water. Maybe I've exaggerated a little; there are some locals at my home break who are more than willing to share their waves, but it's definitely not the majority. However, if every local surfer was as stingy as I portrayed—loathing every new person who shows up at their beach—wouldn't it seem unfair? It's not like a person can own the waves, at least I've never heard of anyone buying the ocean. It's free to everyone, professional and novice surfer alike, so it doesn't seem fair that some of us can act like we have the right to hoard all the good waves, essentially using what's not ours to begin with for our own advantage. Maybe the problem begins with the way we talk about where we surf: MY home break.

It's sad to imagine that waves have been turned into possessions to use at one's own dispense, yet I'm even more troubled when I consider the same or worse is happening with humanity's use of God's creation. God created the earth and everything in it, on it and around it as perfect as it could be, and then He trusted humanity to look after it and enjoy all its goodness. God didn't hand over the rights of creation to humanity as an inheritance, nor did God sell it to us at a high price. God has blessed us by letting us walk and breathe and live as part of God's good creation, and as a bonus appointed us the privilege of taking care of it. We don't own creation, and it's not ours to do with as we please. Creation is meant to be cared for, shared, and enjoyed according to the will of the one who created it: God. We are simply God's stewards.

I know the word "steward" isn't a part of our everyday vocabulary. Maybe the only time you've heard it spoken was during a stewardship campaign at your church, and the only thing you remember was the pastor talking about finances. It's true that God expects us to be good stewards of our money, but stewardship means so much more.

A steward is someone who's been entrusted with something to be used in a way that is pleasing to the owner. A steward isn't given the freedom to do with it however he or she pleases, but with the understanding that it will be used according to the will of the one who has given it. It's not like a rent-to-own agreement, where the person renting does what they want because they know someday they'll own it anyway. A steward isn't given the option to own the thing. Actually, they are expected to return it in the same condition or better than when they received it. The understanding of a steward gets confused at this point, because the focus easily becomes solely on one's responsibility to return it. When this happens, it is forgotten that what we do with it until the time comes to give it back matters just as much. A steward's responsibility to use it according to the owner's wishes is as important as giving it back.

We are God's stewards of creation. We've been entrusted to care for and use creation according to God's will. We have no right to dispose of the earth or the rest of creation however we want, but only as it pleases God. Nothing belongs to us; there isn't one thing we can call our own. It sounds like a chore or maybe a hidden curse, but it's not. Of every living thing that God made, God chose us to look after the rest of creation. I guess it could have been worse. Can you imagine a prairie chicken taking care of creation? God loves us enough to trust us to be in charge of everything.

There will come a time when we'll no longer be God's stewards, and at that time, we'll be asked to describe the type of steward we were while living on earth. Did we look after creation in a way that is pleasing to God, or did we use creation according to our own desires?

I'm not saying that we need to work our way into heaven by being a good steward. What I am saying is that God has a purpose for creation that includes humanity, and when you accept Christ into your life, God starts to reveal that purpose to you. Not only does God reveal things to you, but God begins to shape you into the person who will do those things. It's nothing you can do on your own power, but it's what God does in you that enables you to do God's will. If you have a relationship with God and are open to what God wants to do in your life, then you don't need to worry; God will give you the strength to be a good steward.

Not every person who believes in God is willing to be shaped by Him.

If people don't allow God to be active in their lives, then it's impossible to live in a way that's pleasing to Him. God can't reveal to us our role as stewards of creation if we are not willing to listen.

Our eternal reward isn't based so much on our work as it is on God's work in us. When God is free to work in your life, you will become the person God is calling you to be. The moment God inquires, you'll be able to tell a good story of caring for creation.

I must admit, I'm concerned that many of us treat creation like the local surfers I described earlier in the chapter treat waves. We treat it like creation is all "mine," and nobody else has a right to it except me. We're not willing to share creation with anyone else. Instead, we gather and use as much of it as possible for our own pleasure. Some of us definitely aren't willing to invite others to enjoy creation the way we do, especially if it will take away from our own happiness. Our use of creation is all about "me."

I'm concerned that some of us are missing out on our call to be God's steward. We think we own the place, so we can do whatever we want with it. We're willing to drain creation's resources to create a better world for ourselves, regardless of how it affects the environment now and for future generations. The way we use creation has everything to do with our own desires and little to do with God's will. For those of us who desire to be restored into the image of God, however, we realize "we cannot be 'wise stewards' unless we labor to the uttermost of our power; not leaving anything undone which we possibly can do, but putting forth all our strength."[18] It's not about *my* home break or *my* earth; it's about caring for creation in order to please the one who entrusted it to us.

CHAPTER 10
GLOBAL SURF
ESCHATOLOGY

The best wave I've surfed might qualify as mediocre at beaches in places such as Hawaii, Fiji, and Australia. It's not so much a statement about my ability as it is a reality of where I've surfed—the east coast of Florida. Florida's east coast isn't known for big, gnarly waves like most of you have seen on television or on the cover of surfing magazines. There are worse places in the world to live as a surfer—like in the middle of Ohio—but Florida doesn't boast the world's best waves. Don't get me wrong. I love surfing in Florida, it's the place where I fell in love with the sport. Plus, it is home to the world's only seven-time world champion surfer, Kelly Slater. Florida is my home, but other parts of the world host bigger, faster, and closer-to-perfection waves. Global surf is where it's at.

In search of the perfect wave, surfers for decades have been scrounging up every last penny they could find under their bed and in between their couch cushions to pay for a surf trip to some of the most remote parts of the world. The home break is where one goes to surf a familiar wave, and the rest of the globe is where one goes to find and surf the perfection. It's part of every surfer's dream to travel to a corner of the world where no other surfer has been before and surf the most epic wave that ever existed with no one else around but their friends. Traveling around the world to surf is such a big deal that several people have made a business out of starting companies solely for assisting one's surf travel needs. (If you don't believe me try an internet search for "Surf Express.")

Surfing isn't like basketball, football, baseball, or even soccer where professional leagues are limited to one country or at least one continent. Professional surfers can't just hop on a bus or catch a short plane ride to their next event, because their next destination may be halfway around the world. The travel schedule of the world's best surfers resembles the experience of contestants on the popular reality TV show "The Amazing Race," which often involves boarding a plane in Africa and arriving at their final destination in Fiji—all in less than 24 hours. Not only do professional surfers chase events all over the world, but they take an occasional detour along the way to catch a surprise swell of the decade off the coast of who-knows-where before heading to their next scheduled stop. Surfing is truly a global experience.

Like I said, I've only been blessed with the excitement of waves off the coast of east central Florida. However, that doesn't mean that I haven't dreamed. I've literally dreamed that I was riding the tube at Pipeline in Maui, where I cruised down the line of a hollowed-out wave until it finally shot me out the other end like a barrel of a shotgun. I've dreamed, while admiring the photos in the latest surf magazine, of the day when I would paddle out in waters lined up with wave after wave of perfection. I once shared this dream with a friend, until the day when I received a phone call.

I didn't recognize the number on my cell, and I normally don't answer if I don't know who it is, but for some reason this time I flipped it open and said hello. Usually I'm good at recognizing voices on the phone, and he obviously thought I knew his, but for some reason it just wasn't coming to me. I had no idea who was calling me. The voice said, "Guess where I am?" Since I had no clue who it was, I responded with, "I have no idea." His answer: "I'm in Puerto Rico." That was it, that's all I needed to know to realize who was on the other end of the phone. I couldn't believe my own ears: Brandon was in Puerto Rico on a surfing trip with some of his buddies, and I was left in Florida to hear about it.

We made a promise to surf in Puerto Rico someday, and when I say "we", I mean Brandon and me. Brandon was a student in Brooklyn's youth ministry, but he was also the person most willing to go surfing with me almost any time I called. (Yes, I'm talking about the same Brandon who surfed with me the day after the hurricane.) Though it was probably craziest surf experience we shared, it definitely wasn't the only. I could write page after page of our surf adventures that would cripple you with both laughter and fear, but sadly, all of them would share one thing in common: Florida's east coast. It's not so much sad for you, but sad for us because our wave experience is limited to less than perfection. So we made a commitment to surf somewhere else, somewhere not on the east coast of Florida.

Well, as you already know, Brandon left me dreaming while he took the first of what would be many global treks to find the perfect wave. Brandon has joined thousands of surfers who have set out on a quest to travel to even the furthest corner of the earth to surf waves that can only be imagined in one's dreams. He traversed the boundaries of a local surfer and became a foreigner, all for the sake of finding a better wave. His eyes have now been opened to the beauty and excitement of a coastline beyond the sixty-mile stretch from Cocoa Beach to Sebastian Inlet, to a surf world without end. When Brandon thinks of surf, he can imagine a place other than Second Light in Cocoa Beach.

Global surf is about imagining the value of a coastline that is unfamiliar, faraway, and rarely considered. It's about opening yourself up to the goodness of all parts of the world, even in places with sub-zero temperatures. Everywhere water exists is a possibility to ride a unique wave, just ask the people who surf Lake Erie or rivers in Europe or the beaches of Canada. It's about finding the good all over the earth, not just the place we call home.

Creation is moving toward a global renewal. It sounds crazy, I know, but it's true. It's found in Revelation 21:1 where the Apostle describes to us his vision: "And I saw a new heaven and a new earth," and then in 21:5 God says from the throne, "Behold, I am making all things new." God cares about all of creation and promises to make it new. Global redemption is where it's at.

Global renewal doesn't really fit what most of us have been taught about the end of the world. When the majority of us consider the end, we have visions of apocalyptic chaos where everything goes wrong and people are struggling to survive. We think of the pearly gates of heaven and the Book of Life that will record all of our past sins. We think of the time of judgment when God will determine whether we make into heaven or will be sent to hell. We think of a red devil with pointy horns and a pitchfork standing in the flames of hell. We think of the streets of gold and angels standing all around signing praises to God, twenty-four seven. To be honest, when most of us consider the end of times, not many think about a new heaven and a new earth.

When it comes down to it, most of us have been trained to focus solely on the fate of our souls. The only thing we've heard about the end is that we better be ready to go to heaven. Nothing else matters; our only hope is an eternity in heaven. I'm not saying it's bad to be prepared to spend eternity with God in heaven, but God has promised so much more.

When we fail to recognize God's promise for all of creation and not just our souls, our actions reflect a selfish neglect of the earth. If the only thing that will be saved is our souls, then there's no time to mess around saving the earth that will someday cease to exist. At least, that's how our thought processes work.

Why bother caring for creation if this is as good as it gets? Imagine if Brandon and thousands of other surfers thought the same thing about surfing. They would miss out on thousands of perfect waves breaking all over the world—all because they're not willing to be open to a global perspective. If every surfer thought their home break was as good as it gets, then I would feel bad for those whose home break is on the beaches of Lake Erie. What a sad thought, for surfers to miss the *global* because they're blinded by the *local*. How sad it is that so many people, including Christians, never experience the hope of global renewal because we're too focused on our own future.

God promises to make you a new creation, but God also promises to make creation new. God begins the process of making us new creations now, while we're still on earth. God desires for us to join in the process of making creation new now, while we're still here on earth. As children of God, we live in expectation of what creation will be someday and not what it is now. We look forward to the day when all of creation will be made new, and we care for creation today like it has already happened. We know creation isn't as good as it can be, and we do everything we can to make it like new. Our individual salvation no longer blinds us to global redemption, so we're able to experience the beauty and splendor of caring for creation with the hope that it will some day be perfect again.

All of creation has hope for a new day.

"He that sitteth upon the throne will soon change the face of all things, and give a demonstrative proof to all his creatures that 'his mercy is over all his works.' The horrid state of things which at present obtains will soon be at an end. On the new earth no creature will kill or hurt or give pain to any other. The scorpion will have no poisonous sting, the adder no venomous teeth. The lion will have no claws to tear the lamb; no teeth to grind his flesh and bones. Nay, no creature, no beast, bird, or fish will have any inclination to hurt any other. For cruelty will be far away, and savageness and fierceness be forgotten. So that violence shall be heard no more, neither wasting or destruction seen on the face of the earth."[19]

As those who are being made into the image of God, there's no need for us to wait until that day comes. Through our actions of caring for creation, we can offer glimpses of a promised reality where everything will be made new. No more exploiting creation, no more trashing the earth, no more destroying the environment, no more wasting resources, and no more selfishness.

Surfing is a global thing, and so is God's promise of redemption. God cares enough about creation to promise to make it all new. The question is, will we reflect God's concern for creation and its renewal by the actions that we take to care for it, or will we reject the goodness of creation by continuing to abuse it due to a lack of concern or even blatant neglect? Try to imagine what creation will be like when it's all made new, and then do your best to live like that reality already exists today.

SECTION THREE

FOLLOWING THE FORECAST

CHALLENGE

TO TAKE ACTION

It's easy to believe in something; however, it's not as simple to do something about it. I can't tell you how many people I know who believe they're surfers, but when you put a board in their hand and point them toward the water, they run the other way. In the previous section, I asked you to believe God is calling you to love creation. If you've made it this far, my guess is that you're willing to believe, and more importantly, are ready to do something about it. In this final section of the book, you'll learn what it means to do something about caring for creation.

In this part of the book most of what you'll find is the practical stuff—the how-to of taking action. You'll learn about the what, the how, the when, and the where of caring for creation. By the end, you should be equipped with a plan and the know-how to create a lifestyle of loving creation with your actions.

At this point, I'm working under the assumption that—deep in your heart—God has filled you with a desire for perfection and you're willing to do whatever it takes to find it, even if it means doing something everyone else thinks is crazy. I'm assuming you're like every surfer in search of the perfect wave: you're constantly thinking about how to find it and restless until you do something about it. Staying where you are while everyone else edges closer to perfection isn't enough; you must be in motion. God is filling your heart with love, and you're ready to take action.

It's important to follow the forecast. I'm sure you've seen the weather forecast on your local news channel. Well, surfers also check a wave forecast nearly everyday. Thanks to the internet, surfers can check several websites with daily wave conditions and predictions, including live shots of the beach. Other than a few old school surfers, I don't know any surfer who gets ready and hauls their board to the beach without first checking the forecast. By perusing all of the different web forecasts, a surfer can determine wave height, wind speed, period of swell, time of high tide and low tide, and just about anything else there is to know about waves. Not only can one learn about the current waves, but the forecasts provide wave analysis for each day up to a week ahead of time. The purpose of all of this is to come up with a plan of action.

Not many of us can afford the gas or the time it takes to get to the beach only to find out the waves are horrible. Instead, we check the forecast to help us plan which beach to go to, at what time, with what board, and whether or not to bring the wetsuit. Following the forecast reduces frustration. In your pursuit of perfection, I want to help you realize the beauty of following the forecast on caring for creation. I believe creating a plan of action that fits the forecast will reduce the likeliness of feelings of failure and frustration. Following the forecast will include: (1) Assessing the needs, (2) Choosing which actions to take, and (3) Taking action.

CHAPTER 11

CHECK THE REPORT
ASSESSING THE NEEDS

I can't tell you which website has the best surf report. However, checking the report used to be so simple for me when I thought only one existed. For my first year or so of surfing, I only visited one website. I'm not even sure how I found out about it, but somehow it became a part of my normal routine. I developed a nightly ritual of checking the surf report for the next day, even if I knew I wouldn't be able to go. For some weird reason, I needed to know what the waves would be like tomorrow. Plus, I loved checking out the current day's pictures. I'm not sure who it is, but somebody goes out to the beach super early every morning and takes a picture of the waves. Occasionally, they go back later in the day to take another picture of the same waves with a little more daylight. I don't know why—maybe I'm a little crazy—but I love to see those pictures every day.

The days of simple surf reports are over for me. I would like to accredit it to my improved ability to read a wave, but that would probably be less than the truth. I can't tell you the exact moment my favorites grew from one website to five, but it happened. Almost instantly, my nightly ritual of checking the surf forecast grew from a five-minute exercise to a 15-20 minute one.

Now that I check five forecasts, the task of developing a plan of action is more complicated. It wouldn't be so bad if all the websites agreed in their forecast, but that rarely happens. Each person behind the individual forecasts has their own personality, some very optimistic and others very pessimistic. One website will tell you to grab the board and get to the beach as fast as you can, while another will warn you not to waste your time driving to the beach. Then you have the forecast provided by a website operated by surfers in a completely different country, which provides a completely technical version of what to expect. Most of the time, it's hit and miss with these predictions. The forecast that's always on the positive side has been accurate at times, and the report that leans more on the negative side has been right on the money in the past. I've learned the reality of it all exists somewhere in the middle.

Creating a surf plan may be more complicated and time-consuming, but I am definitely more informed. When I relied on one website report alone, it was either right or wrong. The wave conditions were either exactly like the report said, or they were nothing like the predictions. By checking five forecasts, I get the good and the bad, which helps paint a more realistic picture of what to expect. I know that somewhere between the best and the worst report is the truth. If I'm okay with surfing the worst conditions and good enough to surf the best conditions, then I know how to make a plan.

I put a lot of trust in website surf forecasts, but—realistically—none of them can compare to a face to face encounter with the beach. We have amazing technology to help us read the ocean and make predictions, but nothing can take the place of standing on the beach and seeing for yourself what's happening. The live webcams and still pictures of the beach are awesome, but none of this compares to taking in the scenery with your own eyes. The most reliable forecast is you and what you see.

Caring for creation with our actions requires that we check the forecast, that we assess the needs around us. How do we know what to do, where to begin, or what to expect if we don't know the needs of creation? It's difficult to come up with a plan of action when you have no clue what needs to be done. I guess we could ignore the reports on what's happening in creation and do our own thing, but I think we'd run into more frustration than success. It just seems crazy to plan to go surfing without getting some advice, so why would it be any different when making a plan to love creation with our actions?

I'm not an expert surf forecaster, nor am I an expert environmentalist, and my guess is, neither are you. The good news is that we don't need to pretend to be, because there are plenty of people who are. Just about anywhere you look you can find resources that will inform you of the needs of creation, including ways to get involved. The information is out there waiting to be discovered. Here's how to check the forecast:

Find someone who's already involved. It may be a friend, a pastor, a teacher, a relative, or someone you've never met before; it doesn't really matter. You're looking for someone with passion and experience. This person needs to be someone who has an obvious excitement for doing whatever it takes to care for creation, regardless of how crazy it seems. It should be someone with a clear understanding of our ability and responsibility to act right toward creation. Not only should this person be aware of the needs of creation, but he or she should have already made protecting it a part of everyday life. This person should have been involved in many projects and initiatives to care for creation before, and should now be actively seeking new ways to live responsibly at home, at work, at church, and in the community. He or she should be a veteran of creation care.

It's difficult to start doing almost anything by yourself without eventually reaching the breaking point. It definitely helps if someone is there to help coach and encourage us along the way. I know it's true for surfing. I mentioned earlier in the book that surfers aren't too willing to share pointers and tips to a beginner surfer, especially if they don't know you. They definitely aren't the type to be cheering you on to catch a wave if they think they have a chance to drop in before you do. Unless you know an experienced surfer who's willing to teach you, you're pretty much on your own. Unfortunately, the normal result of teaching one's self to surf is frustration, eventually leading one to give up.

Finding someone who's already committed to Environmental Holiness is essential to a healthy beginning. Their passion and experience have taken them closer to the needs of creation than you can ever imagine, and they will do whatever they can to share it with you. They can tell you the best way to get started, where to go, what to do, and how to plan for the next step. Without a partner, it's much more difficult to discover the needs of creation and initiate a plan of action.

Discover reliable resources. Several books have been written and websites created on the topic of creation care, in addition to the numerous magazines and newspaper articles committed to the environment. Thanks to the internet, you're only a few key words and clicks away from a number of websites committed to taking care of creation. Plus, most local libraries have moved to an electronic catalogue, so you can look up books and check your MySpace at the same time. I guess you could order a book from an online bookstore, but for the sake of saving paper and money, I would encourage you to check it out from the library. You'd be learning about caring for creation and actually doing it at the same time.

I use the word "reliable" to describe the type of resources I'm encouraging you to find for a reason. Not all the resources you come across will be helpful or truthful, especially on the internet. I'm sure you'll even stumble on a few that will discourage the need to care for creation. I don't have the space to discuss which resources are good and which should be avoided, but here are a few questions to ask yourself:

- Is the resource written from a Christian perspective? Not every good resource is written from the viewpoint of a Christian, but it's a good place to start. It's important to learn from others who are motivated by God's love and a relationship with Christ. I will warn you, however, that not all Christian resources are in favor of caring for creation.

- Who published the resource? Choose books with a publisher you know and trust. Don't be too afraid to try new publishing houses, but if nobody has ever heard of it before, then it's probably not the most reliable. With internet resources, it takes a bit more effort to find out the publisher. Each website should have a section about their history and/or statement of belief. If you can't find either one, then move on to the next search result. If the websites aren't willing to identify who they are, what they believe in, and what they've done, then the level of legitimacy decreases drastically.

- Is the resource supported by anyone? It could be a church, a university, an organization, the government, or even an individual. If it is, then it's important to find out as much as you can about the sponsor(s). What you learn about the sponsoring organizations will tell you a lot about the resource itself. Choose resources with sponsors you know and trust.

- Is the author committed to caring for the creation? Not every book will enthusiastically support you in your goal of protecting creation, so make sure what the author's position is before you take to heart everything he/she says.

Get face to face with creation. Like I said, no surf forecast can replace the advantage of standing on the beach and seeing it with your own two eyes. Words can't express nor can pictures capture what you can experience standing right in front of the waves. The same is true with creation. Nothing can tell you more or help you plan to act better then experiencing the needs of creation firsthand. Sure, you can read and hear about it from others, and I've encouraged you to do so. The awareness you'll receive when you stand in the presence of real needs, however, can't be replaced. When you're right there and experience the pain of creation for yourself, the things you can do to help come much more clearly into focus.

What I mean by getting face to face with creation is simply observing how the way you, your family, your school, your church, your community, your state, and your country treat the earth. It could be as simple as determining how many houses in your neighborhood recycle, followed by a trip to your nearest landfill. "Paper accounts for 40 percent of all the waste dumped into our landfills,"[20] so just imagine what would happen if we recycled. Getting face to face with creation is more than relying on someone else's word; it's actually seeing it for yourself.

Now that you know how to check the forecast and realize the needs of creation, it's time to move on to the next step: choosing which actions to take.

CHAPTER 12
CHOOSE A LOCATION
CHOOSING WHICH ACTIONS TO TAKE

Choosing which beach to surf is like choosing ice-cream; it's a dilemma between playing it safe by going with the favorite or taking a risk by trying something new. It really shouldn't be so difficult, but somehow it always is. Something inside of me and most other surfers won't allow us to drive straight to our favorite spot without stopping at all the breaks along the way. I admit it's a bit compulsive, but we do it anyway. We do it because we're afraid to miss out on a better swell, even though we check the same spots everyday and know how they break. Ninety-nine percent of the time, our favorite break produces the best waves according to our individual tastes, but most of us can't look past the other one-percent. We spend an extra thirty to forty-five minutes checking all the spots along the way, so we can feel at peace that we're not missing out on the one percent chance that the waves are better somewhere else.

I wish things didn't have to be so complicated, but with so many beaches lining the coast, it's difficult to choose. I always check the forecast ahead of time, which really helps, but when it comes down to it, I have to choose. I can't experience all the beaches in one day; there's not enough time in the day nor do I have the energy to pack, unpack, and repack that many times. Realistically, I could try several beaches, but there's always the possibility that my timing would be off at every new break. I could show up a bit too early or late to catch the best waves of the day at every spot. So even if I did decide to go from beach to beach, it's still a gamble. As tough as it can be sometimes, I have to choose a location.

Choosing which actions you take to care for creation can be as complicated as choosing ice cream or which beach to surf. Once you've started checking the forecast on the needs of creation, it won't take you long to realize that it can be overwhelming. The needs of creation are everywhere and involve nearly every part of our lives. The opportunities for you to take action are as numerous as all the beaches in the world combined. It's close to impossible for you to do them all, and if you could, you probably wouldn't be able to carry the burden long without major burnout or meltdown. If you're like me, you're the type of person who doesn't want to miss out on an opportunity, which makes it a difficult choice. It's not bad to have a desire to do all you can, but it's important to know that at some point, you have to choose. To be the most effective caretakers of creation we can possibly be, we need to choose which actions to take.

I want to give you a strategy to help you know how to choose which actions to take in your commitment to care for creation. When we don't have a strategy, it's easy to be here, there, and everywhere while at the same time not being anywhere. It's not hard to jump into something head first and when you come to the surface realize you're in too deep. I believe we can avoid some of the stresses and frustrations of caring for creation if we had a strategy to help us choose which actions to take.

The strategy that I'm about to give you is simple. It involves breaking our actions into five different areas: (1) Personal Actions, (2) Family Actions, (3) Church Actions, (4) Community Actions, and (5) Global Actions. The strategy is to choose actions that fit into each of the five areas. I told you it's simple. Okay, maybe it gets slightly more complicated because you still need to choose from many possibilities in each area. Don't worry! I will help you with those choices. The main point of the strategy is for you to avoid getting overwhelmed with one of the main areas by intentionally focusing on all five. Here's how it works.

START WITH PERSONAL ACTIONS

Begin with you and what you can do. Personal actions are the things we can do as individuals right *now*. Does it seem overwhelming? I'm not implying that you alone should solve every environmental issue. However, what I am saying is these are individual actions you can do *now*, right where you are. Keep this in mind: it's up to you and no one else.

There are so many possibilities for personal actions that you could spend the rest of your life chasing them all, but that's not what I'm suggesting you do. Instead, you need to ease your way into a personal lifestyle of caring for creation. Choose one personal action at a time. It doesn't matter what it is, it's up to you. You'll be tempted to choose more than one, but don't. Here's why: your goal is for the personal action to become a natural part of your lifestyle for the rest of your life. For however many years you've been alive, you've lived a certain way, and now all of a sudden you've decided to change. Change isn't easy, especially if it means breaking a habit you've had your entire life. To give yourself the best chance to make it stick, choose one new personal action at a time. When you've performed the action successfully for one month, then you can move on to the next one. You may be successful the first month, or it may take two or three; it doesn't matter. If you can do it for a month, chances are you will do it the rest of your life.

Here are some ideas for personal actions:

- **Give up bottled water.** No, you don't need to give up water, but you will need to stop drinking it from a plastic bottle. You can still drink water on the go; it just needs to be in a non-toxic reusable bottle. For those disgusted by tap water, you should know that 40 percent of bottled water sold in the United States is actually tap water (fooled me). Not to mention the fact that tap water costs about a penny a gallon, while bottled water costs close to $10 a gallon. Honestly, it's not about the difference between tap and bottled water, it's about creating a habit that is good for the environment. You should know that it takes somewhere around 1.5 billion barrels of oil to manufacture plastic bottles in the United States, which is enough to power 100,000 cars. For the big kicker: 86% of plastic bottles in the United States never get recycled.[21] Americans go through 2.5 million plastic bottles every hour, and five of the top six chemicals on the EPA's list of chemicals that produce the most hazardous waste during production are used by the plastics industry.[22] I don't know how many millions of plastic bottles aren't recycled, but I'm sure the earth's soil isn't happy being packed with thousands of them every day. Kick the bottled water craze!

- **Bag packaging.** Refuse to accept plastic packaging at the store by bringing your own earth-friendly, reusable bag. In Los Angeles alone, residents use more than 6 billion one-time plastic bags a year, and only 5 percent are recycled.[23] Guess what happens to the other 95 precent? Yep, most of it ends up crowding the landfills. For those that don't make it to a landfill, they pose a threat to our rivers, lakes, and other natural habitats, including the fish and animals that so easily become entangled in them. In the U.S. alone, it's estimated that we go through about 100 billion plastic bags a year.[24] If you do the math, then 95 billion plastic bags pollute the creation every year, and that's just the United States. Carry your own bag or backpack to the grocery store or any other place you shop—including the mall—and refuse to walk out of the store with plastic.

- **Cut paper out.** Or at least reduce the amount of paper you use. Do everything you can to avoid using paper at home, at school, at work, or wherever you are, and if you must, use recycled materials. Don't forget to recycle what you do use. It's hard to imagine, but it takes an entire forest (over 555,000 trees) to support one Sunday's newspaper consumption across the U.S.[25] We could read the same newspaper on the internet, which would spare 52 forests and 28,860,000 trees every year. If you are forced to use paper, like for an assignment at school, use recycled paper to help reduce the rate of deforestation. Seventeen trees are saved for every ton of high quality recycled paper used, in addition to saving 7,000 gallons of water and 60 pounds of air pollution.[26] Do whatever it takes to limit your paper use, which includes toilet paper, facial tissues, paper towels, books, magazines, newspapers, copy paper, notebook paper, posters, and on and on. Find a creative alternative to paper.

EASE INTO FAMILY ACTIONS

I say ease, because now you're dealing with more than just your own life. As excited as you may be, there's no guarantee that the rest of the family will feel the same way. If you move too fast and push too hard, they may end up making you a bed in the doghouse. Your goal isn't to create chaos and mayhem in your house by changing your family's lifestyle overnight. Instead, your purpose is to influence your family to accept the responsibility to care for creation and initiate patterns of living that will become a natural part of your family's everyday existence. It doesn't take much to overwhelm a family with lifestyle changes, which normally results in frustration and failure. Take it easy, move slow, and your family will begin to see the beauty of caring for creation.

Family Actions are the lifestyle choices your family and you can make to care for creation. They aren't actions your family should feel forced to do. They are simply commitments your family is free to make to do whatever you can as a group to show concern for creation. It's a family thing, and only your family can decide to do it. Take a look at some ideas for Family Actions:

Use water wisely. This includes conservation and protection, both of which can help slow down water scarcity and prevent water pollution. Most of us in the United States don't worry about running out of water or having access to safe water, but a large portion of the rest of the world does. Over 40 percent of the world's population lives in conditions of water scarcity and polluted water, and it is projected to grow to 50 percent by 2025.[27] Over one billion people lack access to safe water, and close to 2 billion lack safe sanitation.[28] Your family can do something about these problems by conserving water and preventing water pollution.

Check out these helpful tips:

1. Check for hidden leaks or toilet leaks.
2. Don't use the toilet as a wastebasket.
3. Install water-saving shower heads and low-flow faucet aerators.
4. Take shorter showers.
5. Turn off the water after you wet your toothbrush.
6. Use your dishwasher and clothes washer for only full loads.
7. Don't leave the water running for rinsing dishes.
8. Turn the hose off in-between rinses when washing the car.
9. Choose plants that don't require a lot of water.
10. Harvest your rainwater and grey water.
11. Don't pour hazardous chemicals down the drain, inside or outside.

(You can find other helpful tips at www.eartheasy.com/live_water _saving.htm or www.treehugger.com/files/2006/12/how_to_green_your _water.)

Make your home energy efficient. It's about not wasting energy. Your family can cut back on the amount of energy you use and still benefit from the same services as before. Because a large amount of the energy in the United States is generated from burning coal, saving energy leads to less pollution in the air and in the water. In using less energy, your family can do something positive to counteract the pollution that contributes to global climate change and threatens the ecosystem of lakes, rivers, and other natural bodies of water.

Here are some ways to save energy at home:

1. Switch to compact fluorescent light bulbs.
2. Turn down the temperature of your water heater.

3. Clean or replace furnace, air conditioner, and heat-pump filters on a regular basis.
4. Turn off and unplug appliances while not in use, including cell phone and computer chargers.
5. Turn off anything that doesn't need to be on.
6. Plant shade trees around your house.
7. Buy appliances with the EPA "Energy Star" label.
8. Use less hot water.
9. Do an energy audit.

Travel smart. Make transportation choices that reduce the negative impact on creation, particularly with the use of your car(s). The United States is the world's largest emitter of greenhouse gases, and the greatest portion of pollution is attributed to transportation.[29] A huge portion of families in the U.S. own at least two cars, some even three. Most of the time, cars are driven with only one or two passengers. Besides this, there are a significant number of large vehicles driven such as SUV's, heavy-duty trucks, and large-size vans, which contribute to the pollution problem by burning fuel at a higher rate. It's not like we're slowing down much, considering that from 1970 to 2000 the vehicle miles traveled in the U.S. increased 149 percent while the population only increased 39 percent.[30]

Here a few suggestions:
1. Choose one day every month to leave your car(s) parked. No driving for 24 hours.
2. Use personal vehicles less. Walk, bike, carpool, or use public transportation whenever possible.
3. When moving to a new location, choose a place close to work.
4. Choose the most fuel-efficient and least-polluting vehicle.
5. Avoid driving a large SUV.

GET INVOLVED WITH CHURCH ACTIONS

I say get involved like your church is already caring for creation, but they may not be. If your church is already involved in creation care, awesome, all you need to do is ask a church leader how to get involved. If your church isn't doing much to care for the earth, then it may be up to you to be the one to help it get started. Don't worry: God will give you the strength and awareness to know how to initiate actions in your church. Plus, I'll provide some resources that can possibly give you a head start.

Church Actions are the things we can do to care for creation that require more than an individual or family to accomplish. They are choices and activities that are only made possible when a church community decides together to do something about the needs of creation. More importantly, they are motivated by God's love filling our hearts and re-creating us in the image of God. A church makes the choice to take action because it understands our responsibility to care for what God has created. There's no selfish or political agenda backing it up; it's about living out of a heart filled with love.

Take a look at some examples:

Get with the program. This is for the churches that don't have a program of creation care already in place. Every church needs to establish a program or strategy to help inform and engage its members in creation-care efforts. How else is everyone expected to know what to do or how to get involved? Fortunately, you don't need to be the one to develop the program, because other churches have already done it for you. All you need to do is check out their programs and decide which one best fits the personality of your local church. Just a note: be sure to ask a key leader to partner with you.

Here are a couple examples of church programs:

1. Greening Congregations Program & Greening Congregations Handbook (www.earthministry.org, Cultivating Congregational Involvement).

2. The Green Congregation Program (www.webofcreation.org).

Worship the Creator. Your church can make a commitment to acknowledge God as Creator and recognize our responsibility to care for creation in worship services throughout the year. Through the worship experience, your church community can praise God for being the Creator of all things, celebrate the value of everything in creation, confess our sins against creation, mourn the sufferings of creation, and commit yourselves to care for the earth and all its inhabitants. The goal or purpose isn't to make it a one-time event, but to create an identity where caring for creation is an integral theme easily recognized in our worship experiences throughout the year. Here are a few suggestions:

1. Celebrate a Season of Creation. A season of four weeks where we can celebrate God as Creator and the life of the created order in four key worship services. Go to www.seasonofcreation.com.

2. Hold a Greening of the Cross Service. Worshipers put greenery on a wooden cross to symbolize how Jesus' death renews all creation.

3. Blessing of the Animals Service (www.webofcreation.org).
4. Create a special worship service for Earth Day/Week.
5. Offer a Covenant with Creation Worship Service. This service gives worshipers an opportunity to sign a "Covenant with Creation" to establish their commitment to do their part in caring for creation.
6. Include prayers, songs, sermons, and art that celebrate creation.

Green the grounds. Develop a plan to reduce the destructive impact your church's buildings and grounds may have upon creation. Decide to make choices that lessen your church's negative effect on creation, and commit to actions that renew and restore the earth and its creatures. Do everything possible to reduce the ecological imprint of your church's building and grounds in regard to all the physical areas of the property. Here are a few suggestions:

1. Do a Comprehensive Environmental Inventory. For a *Comprehensive Environmental Guide*, go to www.webofcreation.org.
2. Change your lighting to compact fluorescent light bulbs.
3. Do an energy audit.
4. Switch to renewable energy.
5. Recycle.
6. Use less paper, plastic, and other non-reusable products.
7. Avoid pesticides, herbicides, and fertilizers with high levels of dangerous chemicals.
8. Grow and sustain a community garden.
9. Plant more trees.
10. Eliminate all vending machines.

JOIN COMMUNITY ACTIONS

I won't say they're everywhere, but most cities and towns should have an organization or group of people who are committed to issues related to caring for creation. You may think you're alone, but chances are there are other people close by who are concerned about the needs of creation and feel a responsibility to take part in reversing the negative impact. They may or may not have a Christian perspective, but that's okay. As long as you do your research and agree with what they are doing, you should be okay. Your goal is to find a group of people in your city or town to connect with who share a concern for the earth in order to open yourself up to new ways to get involved.

Community Actions are opportunities to join with others in your city or town to do something to heal and renew creation. It is a chance to meet with people from all walks of life who share a need to act responsibly by doing something together that is positive for creation. It's a choice to lay aside whatever differences we might have long enough to respond with our minds, hands, and feet to the needs of the earth and all God's creatures. It's an opportunity to unite with others in an effort to heal the wounds of creation in your own backyard.

Take a look at some examples of community actions:

- **Learn the local issues.** Attend rallies, forums, or other public presentations addressing environmental issues in your city or town.
- **Get to know your local officials.** Spend time learning about environmental legislation and familiarize yourself with the elected government officials in your city or town who can influence decisions.
- **Join a local environmental group.** You could ask your science teacher, check the yellow pages, or browse the internet to find an organized group of people committed to issues of creation care.
- **Participate in Earth Day/Week celebrations.** It happens every year in April, so there should be enough time for you to find out all the details or begin planning one for your city or town.
- **Participate in Earth Hour.** Earth Hour started when people in Sydney, Australia decided to come up with a way to inspire others to take action against climate change. So, on March 31, 2007, 2.2 million people and 2,100 Sydney businesses turned off their lights for one hour.[31] Inspired by their actions in Sydney, some of the world's major cities have decided to mark off one hour out of the year to turn off their power. For more information, go to www.earthhour.org.

PARTNER WITH GLOBAL ACTIONS

I say "partner" because most of the time, you won't be able to go to the places that you're seeking to help. Creation is in trouble all over the world, not just in your town, state, or country. Just because it's thousands of miles away, doesn't mean that we don't have a responsibility to do something about it. Those living in a third world country desperately need others from a first-world country to partner with them in an effort to care for creation. Creation in the countries of Africa is as important to God as creation in the United States and Canada, and our actions should reflect that. We have a responsibility to care for all of creation, including the earth, the sky, the universe, and all of space.

Global Actions are the things we can to do to heal the wounds of creation in all parts of the world. In most cases, it will mean partnering with an existing organization committed to a specific need in a particular area of the world. Partnering could mean spending a few weeks or months in another country working with a team of volunteers to overcome a particular issue, or it could be making a financial commitment to support a program or project already in progress. Global actions aren't limited to a partnership, but may also include advocacy or even the power of voting. Whatever it may be, it's a choice to do something about the needs of creation everywhere.

Take a look at some examples:

Buy fair trade products. With a lot of our purchases, we have the choice to buy products that have been produced under conditions detrimental to creation or products produced with a positive ecological impact. It's common for most of the world to buy products based on the least expensive price without considering where or how it was made. Little do we know that prices are often lowered by manufacturing practices that are harmful to creation. It's not always true that cheaper equals more destructive to creation, but price isn't the point. It's about choosing to buy products that limit the negative impact on creation, such as clothing, coffee, tea, and other everyday products.

Here are a couple suggestions:

1. Join the Trade Justice Movement. Check out the following websites:
   www.tradejusticeusa.org
   www.globalexchange.org
   www.usft.org
   www.globaljusticenow.org
   www.oxfamamerica.org

2. Buy from retailers who support trade justice. Go to www.coopamerica.org & www.fairtradefederation.org.

Choose an organization. You may hear about an environmental concern somewhere in Africa and feel compelled to do something about it, but you may be unsure how to get involved. Maybe your eyes have been opened to problems in Guatemala or Thailand, but you don't think there's anything you can do to make a difference. That's not true. There are organizations all over the world whose mission it is to help heal creation, and they want you to be a part of the solution. These organizations have seen the need firsthand, developed a plan, recruited volunteer help, and initiated programs to make a difference for creation in several parts of the world. They've created ways for you to support what they are doing, whether it's giving prayer support, financial help, or becoming a volunteer.

Here are some organizations to consider:

1. *Floresta*. A Christian non-profit organization seeking to reverse deforestation and poverty in the world. Go to www.floresta.org.
2. *A Rocha*. A Christian nature conservation organization. Go to www.en.arocha.org/usa.
3. *New Community Project*. A faith-based non-profit organization promoting peace through justice, care for creation, and experiential learning. Go to www.newcommunityproject.org.
4. *Target Earth*. Their vision is to involve as many people as possible in the service of the earth and the poor. Go to www.targetearth.org.

Be an advocate. You may not think your voice can make a difference, but it can. Maybe your voice alone will struggle to make change, but when joined with thousands of others; it can go a long way in influencing certain policies and laws in the U.S. and throughout the world that hurt creation. For years, people have united their voices in an effort to speak out against injustice. As a result, many new policies have been written, and laws have been changed. As an advocate, you're seeking to change the systems contributing to the degradation of creation by engaging in activities with the potential to influence government policies.

Here are some examples of advocacy:

1. Sign and circulate petitions that support legislative actions and policies friendly to creation.
2. Vote for creation-care. You may not be able to vote, but some day you will. Also, you can influence the way your family votes. Check out www.lcv.org.
3. Make a statement. You can sign a statement to be sent to a government official, such as your state senator, voicing your concern over a particular issue. For an example, go to www.regenerationproject.org and click on 'Take Action.'

Choosing which actions to take is as important as choosing which beach to surf: it can either make it all seem worth it, or it can burn you out to the point of giving up. By following a strategy, I believe you're more likely to find the experience you were looking for while maintaining a constant urge to go do more. The strategy I've given you is simple: (1) *Start* with *Personal Actions*, and then (2) *Ease into Family Actions*. Once you've had time to make lifestyle changes with your family, search for ways to (3) *Get Involved with Church Actions*. Then look for opportunities to (4) *Join Community Actions*, and lastly, (5) *Partner with Global Actions*. Your goal is to choose actions in each of the five areas while keeping in mind that it's okay to take it one step at a time.

It's impossible to do everything all at once, so don't feel the pressure to fulfill each of the five areas within the next five months. Take it easy, don't overwhelm yourself, and trust God to help you choose actions that will change your lifestyle forever.

CHAPTER 13
GET WET
TAKE ACTION

I go to the beach to get wet. My ultimate goal is surfing, but I can't catch a wave if I'm not willing to get wet. I know it will make me sound like a wimp, but it's my least favorite part of surfing. I dread the moment I'm forced to take my first steps into the ocean. I don't know if my skin isn't thick enough to keep me warm or maybe I have a low cold-pain tolerance, but I hate the chilled feeling that washes over me the first 30 seconds I get in the water. It doesn't matter what the air temperature is, I still feel cold every time I jump on my board for the first time. As much as I hate it, I know I need to get wet to surf.

I guess you could say getting wet is the most important part of surfing. It's impossible to surf without at least some part of your body getting wet, even when you wear a wetsuit. There's no way around it. If you take out the getting wet part, then you can forget surfing altogether (and no, surfing the internet doesn't count). You can't be a surfer and stay dry at the same time.

A love for surfing and an appetite to find the perfect wave pushes me beyond my comfort zone to the point where I'm willing to get wet. Honestly, it's doubtful I'd ever get in the water if it weren't for a desire deep inside of me to become a better surfer and chase the crazy idea of a perfect wave. Maybe I'd get in the ocean if I was scuba certified, but I'm not. A search for the perfect wave inspires me to do something I wouldn't ordinarily choose to do, which is get wet.

God fills our hearts with love and begins shaping us into people who reflect the image of God so we can take action. God loves us, so we can love others—including all of creation. Taking action can be as uncomfortable for you as getting in the cold water is for me, but it's also just as important. There's really no way to be a true follower of Christ without the willingness to take action. There's no way around it. If you remove the taking action part, then you might as well forget about reflecting the image of God. It's impossible to have one without the other. God changes us, which changes our actions.

Don't worry; God will give you an appetite for perfection that will inspire you to go beyond your comfort zone to the point that you're willing and even excited to take action. God's love filling your heart and shaping you into the image of God will motivate you to do things that you wouldn't ordinarily choose. It may seem crazy to everyone else, but taking action will be the only thing for you that makes sense.

Every person with a deep desire to find the perfection that only God can give has a responsibility to care for creation. God is waiting for you to get to it, are you willing?

SECTION FOUR
FURTHER RESOURCES
(BOOKS AND WEBSITES THAT CAN HELP YOU LEARN MORE AND GET INVOLVED)

BOOKS BY CHRISTIAN AUTHORS

Caring For God's World: Creative Ecology Ideas for Your Church by Kristen Kemper.

For the Beauty of the Earth: A Christian Vision for Creation Care by Steven Bouma-Prediger.

It's Easy Being Green: One Student's Guide to Serving God and Saving the Planet by Emma Sleeth.

Redeeming Creation: The Biblical Basis for Environmental Stewardship by Fred Van Dyke, David C. Mahan, Joseph K. Sheldon, & Raymond H. Brand.

Saving God's Green Earth: Rediscovering the Church's Responsibility to Environmental Stewardship. by Tri Robinson & Jason Chatraw.

Serve God, Save the Planet: A Christian Call to Action by J. Matthew Sleeth.

Simpler Living, Compassionate Life: A Christian Perspective by Michael Schut.

OTHER BOOKS

Big Green Purse: How to Use Your Spending Power to Create a Cleaner, Greener World by Diane McEachern.

Green, Greener, Greenest: A Practical Guide to Making Eco-Smart Choices a Part of Your Everyday Life by Lor Bongiorno & Frances Beinecke.

Reduce, Reuse, Recycle: An Easy Household Guide by Nicky Scott.

The Green Book: The Everyday Guide to Saving the Planet One Simple Step at a Time by Elizabeh Rogers & Thomas M. Kostigen.

MAGAZINES AND JOURNALS

From a Christian Perspective
Creation Care
Earth Letter
Sojourners

Other Magazines & Journals
Co-Op America Quarterly
Earth Island Journal
E–The Environmental Magazine
The Green Guide

WEBSITES

From a Christian Perspective
www.ausable.org
www.christiansimpleliving.org
www.creationcare.org
www.creationcsp.org
www.nacce.org
www.newcommunityproject.org
www.restoringeden.org
www.whatwouldjesusdrive.org

Other websites
www.futuremakers.com.au
www.planetfriendly.net
www.surfrider.org

ECO-FOOTPRINT CALCULATOR

www.earthhour.zerofootprint.net
www.safeclimate.net/calculator

28. Ibid.

29. "*U.S. Transportation & Global Warming Pollu*tion." <http://whatwouldjesusdrive.org/resources/fs_gw.php>. Accessed April 11, 2008.

30. "*U.S. Transportation & Global Warming Pollution.*" <http://whatwouldjesusdrive.org/resources/fs_gw.php>. Accessed April 11, 2008.

31. "*Where It All Began.*" <http://earthhour.org/about>. Accessed April 11, 2008.

NOTES

1. Mauro, Chris. *"Surf World Shocker: Clark Foam Shuts Down."* <http://surfermag.com/features/onlineexclusives/clarkfoamletter>. Accessed February 12, 2008.

2. Outler, Albert C., and Richard P. Heitzenrater. *"Original Sin", John Wesley's Sermons: An Anthology,* Sermon 44.(Nashville: Abingdon Press, 1991), p. 326.

3. Heitzenratar, Richard. Sermon 6: *"The Righteousness of Faith", Sermons and Hymns of John Wesley,* CD-ROM. (Nashville: Abingdon Press, 1999).

4. Heitzenratar, Richard. Sermon 56: *"God's Approbation of His Work", Sermons and Hymns of John Wesley,* CD-ROM. (Nashville: Abingdon Press, 1999).

5. Ibid.

6. Outler, Albert C. and Richard P. Heitzenrater. *"Original Sin", John Wesley's Sermons: An Anthology.* (Nashville: Abingdon Press, 1991), p. 333.

7. Ibid, p. 334.

8. *"Cruise Ship Pollution."* <http://surfrider.org/srui.aspx?uiq=a-z/cruise>. Accessed February 12, 2008.

9. Ibid.

10. Ibid.

11. Ibid.

12. Ibid.

13. Sermon 139: *"On Love."* <http://new.gbgm-umc.org/umhistory/wesley/sermons/139>. Accessed February 12, 2008.

14. Ibid.

15. Ibid.

16. Sermon 76: *"On Perfection."* <new.gbgm-umc.org/umhistory/wesley/sermons/139>. Accessed February 12, 2008.

17. Heitzenrater, Richard. Sermon 84:*"The Important Question", Sermons and Hymns of John Wesley.* CD-ROM. (Nashville: Abingdon Press, 1999).

18. Outler, Albert C., and Richard P. Heitzenrater. *"The Good Steward." John Wesley's Sermons: An Anthology.* (Nashville: Abingdon Press, 1991), p. 430.

19. Outler, Albert C., and Richard P. Heitzenrater. *"The New Creation." John Wesley's Sermons: An Anthology.* (Nashville: Abingdon Press, 1991), p. 499.

20. *"Surfer Eco Fact: What a Waste."* Surfer. May 2008. Vol. 49, Number 05.

21. *"Why Bottled Water is (Still) Not the Answer."* <http://targetearth.org/about/recycling.html>. Accessed March 18, 2008.

22. *"Refusing and Recycling: It's Our Responsibility."* <http://targetearth.org/about/recycling.html>. Accessed April 11, 2008.

23. *"A Day Without Bags."* <http://c3.newdream.org/blog/2007/12/19/a-day-without-bags/>. Accessed December 19, 2007.

24. Ibid.

25. *"Refusing and Recycling: It's Our Responsibility."* <http://creationcare.org/resources/sunday/facts.php>. Accessed April 11, 2008.

26. Ibid.

27. *"Quick Facts and References: Water Pollution and Water Scarcity."* <http://creation-care.org/resources/sunday/facts.php). Accessed April 11, 2008.